D0757814

CONQUERING LONELINESS

CONQUERING LONELINESS

Harold C. Warlick, Jr.

WORD BOOKS
PUBLISHER
WACO, TEXAS

ISBN 0-8499-0169-3
Library of Congress catalog card number: 79-65189
Printed in the United States of America

*Dedicated to Ruth Babb, "Red" Lewis,
and Lane Mays, who, through Christian
community and meaningful relationships,
turn loneliness into solitude*

ACKNOWLEDGMENTS

The task of thanking those whose help and encouragement made this book a reality is perhaps the project's most difficult chore. First of all, much appreciation is held for Floyd Thatcher, Vice-President and Executive Editor of Word Books, Publisher. Floyd is much more than a prodding and efficient editor. He is a friend whose presence over meals has sharpened many a theological issue.

The desire to tackle the subject came from the constant enthusiasm of my colleague Harvey Cox for my work on Christian community (begun while a student of his), and the encouragement of Judy and Jarrell McCracken whose late-night conversations provided the germs for many an idea.

The work would have remained incomplete without the opportunity extended by Dean Krister Stendahl and the faculty of Divinity of Harvard University to give the Lentz Lecture. Many students and colleagues will also recognize perspectives and questions which arose in fruitful dialogues and classroom exchanges.

Finally, all thanks to Diane and Scott, whose weekends and evenings for an entire year were made more lonely because of this manuscript, and to Posey Belcher, L. D. Johnson, John Killinger, M. B. Morrow, and Robert Noble, my "fathers" in ministry who have made that professional pilgrimage one of joy and meaning.

CONTENTS

INTRODUCTION

WHEN YOU walk down Jones Street in San Francisco around lunchtime, do not be surprised at the mass of humanity surging into St. Anthony's Dining Room. The dining room serves free meals to the poor at the rate of 1,300 every day. The people who file through St. Anthony's to take advantage of the hospitality of the Franciscan brothers reflect in their faces the microcosm of human aimlessness which characterizes our world today.

As part of an urban studies program, I put on old clothes and worn-out shoes and eased into the long line. As we shuffled down the tunnel leading to the kitchen, most of the faces around me stared at the floor. These were the strained, hungry faces of life's losers; the drifting, frustrated faces of the sleepless, resigned to tomorrow's bleakness. Yet out of their common loneliness emerged little hints of community. Little taps on the arm passed among them, signaling at least recognition from another who frequented the same kitchen. A teenage runaway, who appeared to be less than sixteen, eagerly pounced on two

11

cigarette butts found crushed on the ground and shared one of them with the little girl in front of him.

Once inside the huge dining room, I shared a table with a young seaman. He proudly showed me his identification card and talked of distant ports and distant lovers. Each person, seaman included, eagerly devoured the beans, bread, and peppers. One enterprising old couple produced two little plastic bags from their ragged coats and began scraping out leftovers into them. They would not go hungry that night.

Then, as suddenly as the experience had begun for me, it was ended. We got up from the table and made our way back through the tunnel to the streets. I pulled off my dirty, ragged clothes and rejoined the other Baptist ministers from Texas who had been involved in the same experience. Once again I was in my community of Christian friends, and my other luncheon companions were back on the streets. They would fade into alleys and porticos of the city at night, and by day they would gather once again at the doors of St. Anthony's to become a "community" of the lost, lonely, and wretched.

That experience triggered something in my consciousness. It not only made me acutely aware of my reliance on my own Christian community for health, but it opened my eyes to the enormity of human loneliness and the need for meaningful community. We are a nation and a people adrift. We create our gurus, our hostilities, and our stars of the pulpit. From the charismatics who gather in house churches to sing and sway to the corporate executives who kneel and sip the cup of communion from the hands of a priest, from the masses who crowd a huge sanctuary in an event called "revival" to the young people who hold hands and confidently bludgeon others with the "four spiritual laws," we are a people in search of community. We are on the illusory trail of self-gratification. This recognition, triggered by the St. Anthony's food line, gave me the urge to write this book.

Admittedly, the "community" defined in the following pages is a Christian one. I believe the conquering of loneliness can come through a community which in a strange and marvelous way embraces the baptism of Christ, Golgotha, the Resurrection, the Ascension, the Pope marching in solemn procession to St. Peter's, and Luther's burning of the papal bull. Such a community needs to be redefined. We have lost much of our history as a Christian community and cheapened many of its ingredients. Masses of people react to their clergy in a spirit of sullen irresponsibility. Masses of clergy try vainly to keep their churches moving by precise organization and coordination, endless exhortations, and fiscal accomplishments.

Loneliness leaves in its wake a lowering of theological acumen. To speak of loneliness is to speak of peril for the communities of faith. The need for satisfying relationships has stimulated new enterprises, including encounter groups, the electronic church, and a plethora of publications in the grocery stores promising quick, how-to-do-it responses to the problem. Loneliness means big money. It creates a ready market in the publishing field for a lonely-hearts-club approach to religion. Both religion and community have become consumer items. Only in America could we grand capitalists make a profit from the loneliness experience of our culture.

This work is not an attempt to add another superficial twig to the mass-marketing woodpile. It is the attempt to deliver a rather clear and sound message of promise to a society in need of the God of the interpersonal relationship. The promise of affectional bonds in the midst of emotional, social, and existential loneliness is one I wish to convey.

Delivering this message of promise appears to me to be

a proper task for the communities of faith. One might even contend that it is our historical arena. Not surprisingly, other disciplines have given little attention to the pervasive problem of human loneliness. For example, a University of California psychologist, Anne Peplau, compiled a bibliography on the topic that evidenced only 175 articles written on the subject in psychology between 1937 and 1977.

Consequently it appears that even the classical disciplines look to the communities of faith to provide illumination. Well they should, for loneliness demands that a promising word be said not just to illumine our understanding but to illumine our lives as well. This promise is the message of faith.

I share my message with you for, as with Jeremiah, it burns like a fire within my bones and I cannot contain it. The conveyance itself will be my reward, for I have found Joseph Conrad to be right:

> There is no rest for
> a messenger 'til
> the message is delivered.
>
> —*The Rescue*

1.

LONELINESS
and the
Discovery of Strangers

Strangers in Search of Recognition

"Congratulations, you have been recommended for biographical and pictorial inclusion in a volume of the *International Who's Who*. Please send a small paragraph for publication when you return your completed questionnaire. This is the only illustrated *Who's Who* covering your field." So opens the standard form letter, postmarked London, England, which arrives periodically in thousands of homes over the course of a year. And accompanying that letter is a special offer whereby for "only" $150.00 you can obtain a royal edition of the book, or a cheaper paperback copy can be ordered for "only" $50.00.

The success of such offers points to a salient fact in our world: regardless of our position or influence in life, at the most basic level of our existence we are all strangers crying out for recognition, for acceptance, reaching out eagerly for signs of friendship and hospitality.

I believe it was this natural craving of the human heart

which caused Jesus to tell the story of the last judgment as it appears in the twenty-fifth chapter of the Gospel of Matthew. Jesus speaks of the final judgment as a time when humanity is divided into the blessed and the cursed. In reply to earnest petitions from the cursed as to the justification for their status, Jesus answers: "I was hungry but you would not feed me, thirsty but you would not give me drink; I was a stranger but you would not welcome me in your homes, naked but you would not clothe me . . ." (TEV).

The term *stranger*, used by Jesus in this parable of the last judgment, is frequently found in Scripture. It is a Hebrew word that really means "sojourner." Hospitality to the sojourner was recognized as a sacred duty throughout the Mediterranean world. Upon entering a city, a traveler would come to the open place, and there, unless a breach of etiquette occurred, someone would invite him to his home and look after his needs (Gen. 19:1–3; Judg. 19:15–21). The guest was given food, water, and rest, and provision was made for his animals. He enjoyed protection, even if he were an enemy, for three days and thirty-six hours after eating with the host (the time his food would sustain him). This was done because there were no hotels or inns in that period as we have them today. People were literally at the mercy of their society's ability to welcome strangers. Consequently a host never knew when he himself would be dependent on strangers. The societal conditions reinforced the natural craving for fellowship.

Frequently Jesus himself was dependent on the hospitality of others for his daily care and lodging. And later, Christian hospitality was assumed in the sending forth of the apostles. Christians in their travels were to seek out Christian friends, partly for protection but mainly for the sharing of fellowship. In fact, hospitality was the chief bond which united the early churches.

Lest we succumb to the temptation to regard our contemporary society as less dependent upon the hospitality of strangers, consider how our conditions also reinforce that natural craving of the heart for fellowship.

Much of life for many people in our world resembles that of the main character in Albert Camus's first novel, *The Stranger.* That strange little character wanders through life looking in at people from the outside, almost as one looks through a glass. He sees and hears people talking about himself, witnesses their constant shaping of his destiny, yet he is never invited to participate. He notices how everyone is too preoccupied with work and worry to reach out to him in compassion. Finally, his mother dies and he prepares to keep an all-night vigil beside the body, as was the custom during that time in Algiers. The little vagabond notices how all the old folks come in and sit on chairs in the room with him. They all drink coffee which the innkeeper perfunctorily hands out. Throughout the night they simply sip their coffee and look at each other without speaking. The old men sleep hunched up on their chairs while the old women knit and doze. Finally at dawn one of the old men wakes up and coughs repeatedly into a handkerchief. This wakes the others and they all rise to leave. As they depart, each of them stops and shakes hands with the little man and that becomes the only moment of genuine intimacy the character experiences in his entire life.

For some individuals in our society that is analogous to their encounter with higher education. They move through a process whereby people talk about them and shape their destiny without ever inviting their participation. They expend time in a cramped vigil around a body of knowledge, a corpse from past importance, until someone signals that the time of coffee drinking and isolated study is over, shakes their hands, and slaps a diploma on them before departing.

Others shuffle along the well-beaten path of vocational performance until the appointed celebrant coughs not into a handkerchief but a microphone at the company testimonial dinner and offers not only a handshake but a gold watch as well.

And for some, the cough at the end of the vigil is only that of a noncaring, hack nurse pushing them away from children and grandchildren through the corridors of a nursing home, their femininity reduced to the sum total of their child-bearings and miscarriages and serving as a symbol of the weary worlds of popped veins and housework.

These are not pleasant prospects to contemplate. And their terror is heightened when strong relationships which affirm identity become harder and harder to find. As long ago as 1941, Erich Fromm and other personality theorists contended that if society did not meet the basic human needs—for relatedness, transcendence, rootedness, identity, and a frame of orientation—widespread loneliness would result. It now appears that we are perilously close to substantiating that contention. Suzanne Gordon calls loneliness "the new American tradition." [1] In our mobile society the average human being now moves fourteen times in her or his lifetime. A full 55 percent of our adults live over five hundred miles from the place of their childhood roots. When historians write about the '70s and '80s in America, they will refer to loneliness as the characteristic of our period. When we encounter a life-style in which those around us are afraid to risk interpersonal possibilities, incalculable consequences result in our personhoods. We not only become encased in our own loneliness, but we fail to grasp many of the marvelous revelations from God through other people.

The Stranger's Blessing

Most of us do not generally look to strangers for hospitality, let alone for a blessing from God. Rather, we tend to view strangers with suspicion. For good reason, we anticipate hostility, and through words and actions reflect the mood of the day: "Hide your money, lock your door, and chain your bike." We protect our apartments and businesses with dogs and burglar alarms, our roads with anti-hitchhike signs, and our airports with safety officials. We live in a society of hostile strangers. Unfortunately, our retreat from strangers carries as much peril as promise. Jesus expects his disciples to generate hospitality not merely to fulfill the demands of society or even religious valuation, but to recognize the special theological blessings that God has offered and continues to offer through "The Stranger."

The nation Israel had once been a stranger, a sojourner in Egypt, and had been oppressed. She had been a stranger and only the Lord God had taken her in. Yet in taking her in, the Lord God had used her to bless the nations. Consequently, the giving of hospitality is not just a way of blessing the stranger; often by opening ourselves to strangers we find enrichment for our own lives. Scripture is full of such accounts.

A particularly intriguing event took place in the life of Abraham. One day he saw three strangers walking through the desert and invited them to his tent and fed them. The strangers turned out to be angels of the Lord. They informed Abraham and Sarah that at last they were going to have a son. Since Sarah was past the age of child-bearing, this revelation from the strangers was a surprise and shock. But the contribution of the strangers did not terminate at that point—they traveled next to the city of Sodom and just happened to meet a man named Lot who was sitting in the gateway of the city. Lot invited the strangers to spend the night in his home. At first they declined, but Lot was so insistent that they finally accepted his invitation. Following the evening meal, Lot's home was assaulted by an angry mob from the city. They surrounded the house and demanded that the strangers be released to them. Finally, according to the story, the mob dispersed, and the strangers told Lot to take his family and run for their lives because the Lord was going to destroy the wicked city of Sodom. From this we see that great care is taken in Scripture to account for the survival of Abraham and Lot, who had left their country to travel toward the vision of making a great nation, in terms of unexpected blessings from the strangers they had taken in and ministered to.

Even the initial purchase of land in Canaan is the result of the generosity of strangers. Sarah died at the age of one hundred and twenty-seven years in Kiriath-arba, in Canaan. Abraham rose from his mourning and went to the Hittites and said, "I am an alien and a settler among you. Give me land enough for a burial-place, so that I can give my dead proper burial" (Gen. 23: 4–5, NEB).

The Hittites responded by offering Abraham the opportunity to bury Sarah in the best grave they had. Abraham then requested permission to purchase a cave that belonged to Ephron, son of Zohar. After polite negotiations, they came to an agreement on price, and the plot and the cave on it became Abraham's possession as a burial place for his deceased wife.

As I reread the accounts of the beginning of our religion in the life experiences of Abraham, I became fascinated with the way the Lord God kept pushing this wandering nomad toward the promised land through contact with significant strangers.

And this can be true in our society today. When we allow an insensitive, technological culture to rob us of the attitude of welcoming the stranger, we have deprived ourselves of a prominent mode of God's revelation to us. A pivotal element in my own life and ministry has been the powerful personal witness of a man named Jack. On a crisp fall day I was making hospital calls in Anderson, South Carolina. It was Friday afternoon and I was rushing to complete my self-appointed rounds in time to dash back to the church and complete a hastily composed sermon, still "in progress" under a small mountain of notes on my desk. After hurrying through the corridors, rooms, and elevators, I returned to the lobby to replace my chaplain's badge in its rack in the clergy room.

Everything seemed to be running smoothly and on schedule, and it appeared that my sermon would finally receive the needed time and attention. But just when I reached the exit to the parking lot, I felt a hand on my shoulder and a tug on my coat. There behind me stood a member of my church with a rather beleaguered-looking young woman whom I had never seen before. My friend introduced me to her and asked me to pay a visit to her husband, who had just had surgery for cancer. The distraught young woman explained that she and her husband had not gone to church in years but that her husband's surgery had awakened feelings of need on his part, and he wanted to talk with me about God.

I must confess that my mental response to the request was not a good one. These people were strangers, and I hardly had time to call on my faithful church members. Besides, I had played that game of speaking to a stranger so many times before, and it hadn't produced any tangible results. It seemed to me that my church members were constantly asking me to visit various prospects in the com-

munity, and few, if any, of them actually came into the
church. They usually resolved whatever crisis was troubling
them and then went directly back to their pre-crisis life-
style with hardly another thought about the church and
the minister that had seemed so needed at the moment.

Reluctantly I made my way back into the clergy room,
reacquired my badge, and proceeded again through the
corridors as the woman explained her husband's condition.
Jack was thirty-two years of age and had contracted multiple sclerosis six years earlier. He had been a talented man
with an i.q. of 150, who had breezed his way through the
Massachusetts Institute of Technology. His energy and
mental capacities were not consumed by his work as computer manager for a New England oil company, so at age
twenty-five he had designed and built his own race car,
which he subsequently qualified in the Indianapolis 500.
At that time in his life he began to be bothered with
equilibrium problems and a doctor's checkup confirmed
multiple sclerosis. Realizing that his body would quickly
deteriorate, the doctor suggested that he, his wife, and little
boy move to a warmer climate. That's how Jack became a
resident of South Carolina.

I entered the dimly lighted hospital room and pulled a
chair to the bedside of the stranger. He shifted his frail body
underneath the sheets, painfully turned his head to face
me, and without any introduction he said, "I want to become involved in your church and do some church work."
For several moments I sat in amazed silence. Here was a
thirty-two-year-old man recovering from a cancer operation
and who had no use of his arms or legs. In addition, he
barely had vision; he saw only flickering images. And he
wanted to become involved in our church! Sensing my confusion and amazement, he continued, "I have no talent left,
but I will be committed. You can count on me."

I'll never forget the first Sunday Jack came to our church. His wife and child parked their car right in front of the sanctuary, placed Jack in his wheelchair at the bottom of the steps leading to the vestibule, and then honked the horn until the ushers came outside and carried him in. The noise and movement made quite a disruption in the worship service, so several ushers were assigned always to remain outside in anticipation of his arrival. And, week after week, Jack doggedly kept coming.

As time passed, I began to realize that Jack's presence every Sunday was producing some remarkable changes in the church. People who had not attended the services in years because of physical handicaps suddenly began to appear regularly in their wheelchairs and walkers. Others who had stayed away because of health or emotional difficulties began to attend our Sunday morning services. It was an amazing thing to watch—the stranger had set an example that was raising the abilities and expectations of an entire congregation.

Jack's presence also contributed to a redirection of our long-range building needs. For years our church had existed without a sufficient recreation hall and kitchen. And when the time finally arrived to develop designs for a new building for the church, another idea emerged: The sanctuary needed to be remodeled to provide ramps and large corridors to accommodate the increasing number of disabled people who were becoming "involved." Soon we were engaged in an extensive remodeling effort. Jack seemed to find a great deal of pleasure in watching all of these changes take place.

Having helped improve our attitudes and our perspectives, Jack also began to contribute to an improvement in my preaching. As the multiple sclerosis began to take away more of his vision, he looked for new ways to feed his inquisitive mind. He ordered recordings of theology books from the Library of Congress. From these he would extract sermon ideas and quotations and peck them out with a rod stuck between his teeth on his typewriter.

Then, one day the inevitable happened. Jack's body had deteriorated so badly that he could no longer be adequately cared for in his home. He would have to be transferred to a special nursing home a hundred miles away. I assumed that this move would drop the curtain on Jack's unusual influence on our church life. But one day I received a long-distance telephone call from the head nurse in the home where Jack lived. His wife had read the church newsletter to him and he discovered that the next Sunday was the celebration of communion in our worship. He asked, through the nurse, that he be allowed to join us in communion by having some church members bring it to him. In this way he could stay in touch with *his* church, the one that had taken him in while he was a stranger and had given him a home, a place in which to live and love.

Jack's request was honored by our church officials, and each communion Sunday after that a small group drove a hundred miles to carry Jack's communion elements to him. Soon other shut-ins and hospitalized church members had taken cues from the stranger and were making similar requests. It became necessary to organize many people to fan out over the entire city to serve the needs of several dozen shut-ins. This effort energized the congregation and revitalized the religious experiences of the shut-ins.

Our lives were blessed and enriched by this stranger who could not use his arms, legs, and eyes. Indeed, the Christ is often a stranger we welcome into our homes and churches. Hospitality to a sojourner is more than a sacred duty; it is more than gratuity extended to a lonely person.

Often it is opening the door to the finest that life has to offer us.

Sometimes I climb the stairs to my study in my Massachusetts home and stare out the window at the birch trees and snow and think of my friend in the nursing home, now over a thousand miles away. I wonder if the nurses and doctors, as they minister to that feeble body, realize that they are touching holiness. I wonder if God has more blessings and messages wrapped up in that spirit waiting to be opened up by others who would be willing to take in a stranger. And I wonder how many messengers from God pass us each day, intersect our lives and move on without our ever offering to take them into our homes, our personalities, our minds, and our experiences. Perhaps we have within us the capacity to turn our loneliness into solitude, our strangeness into holiness.

Human Contact and Physical Health

The explosion of American life into urbanity and distance from childhood ties has, of course, turned most of *us* into strangers. In our vast sprawling cities, we are perhaps more isolated from meaningful human contact than our ancestors were in rural areas. Chores are no longer social events. Most of us no longer buy food and commodities from people we know. Those strong relationships which affirm our identity are getting harder and harder to find. And our mobile life-style—it is estimated that we'll make fourteen moves in our lifetime—only accentuates our feelings of isolation and aloneness. Consequently, never has there been so much talk of sharing, so many books available on relationships and caring, and so many courses on how to get along with other people. We shout loudest where we hurt the most, and over and over again we reach out to find a place, a person, a church, anything or anyone that can leave us with the feeling that *we belong*.

Our society is finally realizing just how physically devastating loneliness can be. In his book *The Broken Heart*, Dr. James Lynch, a specialist in psychosomatic medicine, probes the medical consequences of loneliness. He believes that those who live secure, stable lives with strong personal ties are far less likely to fall prey to disease than those who live with less human companionship. Fatal heart attacks among widows between 25 and 34 years of age are five times that of married women in the same age group. Among white divorced males, cirrhosis of the liver is seven times more common than among those involved with permanent companions, and tuberculosis ten times more common. The study concludes that unusually close family and community ties help keep down the number of health problems. Lynch says, *"Medical practitioners must make people aware that their family and social life are every bit as important to health as dieting and exercising."* [2]

Loneliness and Aloneness

The kind of loneliness we experience is not a physical state. It should not be confused with the condition which may be called *aloneness*—"not being in the company of other human beings." [3] Loneliness is the result of lack of *purposeful* activity and lack of *purposeful* relationships.

Company does not necessarily cure loneliness. We are all aware of the loneliness of the crowd. Perhaps the greatest loneliness occurs in families as husbands and wives lose sight of their original purposes for being together and try to rush through meaningless activity only to fall headlong into the tunnel of divorce. Loneliness can take place in a roomful of friends who have known each other for years but reflect no shared experiences.

But aloneness, while it can rightfully be differentiated from loneliness, may reveal and increase loneliness and is a factor with which we must come to terms. Physical aloneness aggravates loneliness.

As we glance out our rear window on life into the history of the human race, we see numerous examples that demonstrate how human contact serves as nature's powerful remedy for loneliness. Throughout the winter siege of Leningrad in World War II, the city radio station stayed on the air to reassure people they were not alone. At times the radio announcers became too weak or cold to recite news or play music. They would then turn on a metronome to click monotonously back and forth, echoing through huge loudspeakers in the streets to reassure people that they weren't alone.

Historical accounts of loss of human contact posing as a threat to emotional health are by no means restricted to adults. In the thirteenth century, Frederick II, ruler of Sicily, contended that all people were born with a common language. He suspected that it must have been an ancient language, like Hebrew. To test his theory he devised an unusual experiment. He removed newborn infants from their natural mothers at birth and gave them to foster mothers. He commanded the foster mothers to take care of the physical needs of the babies but never to speak to them. In this way he hoped to learn what language the babies would naturally speak. The experiment failed because all of the children died. They could not live without words, joyful faces, and petting.

Human personality does not emerge out of a social vac-

uum, and it is not sustained in a social vacuum. The poet
W. H. Auden succinctly stated it: "We must love one another or die."

The truth of this statement and our link with the consciousness of history is perhaps attested in an unusual manner in today's technological society. Psychiatrists, social
workers, and the telephone company tell us that in many
large cities thousands of people call the number of the recorded time message to hear the pleasant female voice give
the time. Many dial that number with no thought for the
correct time. They simply want to hear another human
voice.

Physical aloneness is a peril of our time. And it is *not*
the biblical witness. The biblical witness advocates the
creation of affectional bonds in the midst of emotional,
social, and existential loneliness.

If we move beyond the sexist language and implications
of the two creation stories in Genesis, it seems that a rather
clear statement is made that God does not ordain loneliness—paradise is imperfect without meaningful human
companionship. It is not good to be alone. Paradise ceases
to be paradise if in order to obtain it you divest yourself
of human companionship. Consequently the entire biblical
witness treats humankind as community-created and
community-fulfilled. The language is covenant language.
God makes a covenant with humanity and men and women
covenant with each other in meaningful community. The
vision of a messianic banquet unfolds before us. Jesus hammers home the vision of a table at which the poor, the
maimed, the lame, the blind, and all who bear little secular
representation are invited; not the vision of an impersonal
welfare check or food stamps to meet only the bodily needs.
The Kingdom itself is a parent who kills the fatted calf,
brings out the nicest clothes, and spreads a feast for the

homecoming. However we view this Jesus of Nazareth, we must confess that he apparently thought that being separated from the roots of human life, from a community of love, was one of life's most crippling tragedies. Whether by accident, such as a lost coin, or by circumstances such as a lost sheep, or by willful action, such as a prodigal child, to be excluded from the love of human relationships was disaster. That loss of the personal touch, whether you were a leper, an epileptic, a lame person, a prostitute, a mother, or a nomad, was something Jesus sought to rectify, even at the expense of breaking the religious codes and laws of the ages.

Jesus and Physical Contact

Perhaps the pivotal aspect in Jesus' ministry was his affirmation of the importance of human contact and companionship. I strongly believe the significance of Jesus' contact with those who had been diagnosed as lepers cannot be denied. Lepers were not just shunned for fear of contagion. According to the Old Testament law, contact with lepers rendered the holy people of Israel unclean. Regulations imposed a six-foot distance between ordinary people and lepers. Thus a leper was ostracized from the community both socially and religiously.

I have often wondered what motivated Jesus to cross that barrier. What caused him to refuse to love at an arm's length? What factors propelled him toward establishing contacts which would make him "unclean"? What were the moral, emotional, and religious implications of the miracles wrought in the lives of the lepers? Why did he choose physically to touch these strangers?

The history of leprosy in biblical times helps clarify the issue. Originally leprosy was defined in very narrow terms.

The Book of Leviticus described a host of skin diseases which were to be distinguished from leprosy. There were many indications of white spots which broke out on the skin which did *not* render the person unclean. For example, the leprosy of Miriam, the sister of Moses, was of a transient nature, perhaps even psoriasis. Naaman also was permitted to mingle with his own people, indicating that he was possibly suffering from some skin disease other than leprosy. In such instances one was sent to the physician-priest for diagnosis and treatment. It appears that gradually the priests in Israel began to use the terms "clean" and "unclean" to serve as a lever in creating a kind of caste system. As the priests grew more self-righteous, the importance of the ceremonial keeping of the law was heightened. More and more people were forced to live outside the perimeters of meaningful human contact.

As Jesus Christ viewed that destructive process of human isolation, he took an almost unheard-of risk. He made moves toward the unclean and the dispossessed. From Lazarus, to the ten, to the one, Jesus touched those that religious authorities refused to touch. The motif of Jesus reaching out to touch those who had been denied community ran throughout his life, from birth to death. The lepers were the low people on the religious totem pole. They came last in the pecking order of human responsiveness, and they had no home until the Son of Man gave them one.

Aside from the lepers, one other group existed outside the realm of ceremonial religion in the first century. This group also had no religious home. They were the shepherds. To be a shepherd in the first century was virtually synonymous with being unclean simply because, with their lifestyle, they could not meticulously observe the dietary and ritualistic demands of religion. Ceremonial cleansing

was out of the question: they were cast off, ostracized by the
religious community, alone. The only thing worse than being a shepherd was being a leper.

What a shocking thunderclap hit the first century when
the reports came of the birth of the Son of God! To the
shepherds, those wandering, unclean nomads, those lonely,
denied co-occupants with the lepers of the lowest rung in
society's ladder, came these shocking words: "Unto *you*
is born this day in the city of David, a Savior."

The beginning of the life of Christ, his adult ministry,
and his end were all consistent. The message was clear:
strangers are to be touched. Meaningful companionship,
both human and divine, gate-crashed the petty concerns,
structures, and loyalties of history. The alone were to be no
longer alone. The strangers were to be discovered and their
"strangeness" melted away through understanding and
compassion.

That message has been the motivation for many modern-
day saints who have leaped over the barrier of prejudice
and strangeness toward health and wholeness. I think of
Martin Luther King and his somewhat successful efforts to
bring together the black and white strangers in an era of
American history similar to that of Jesus' day, with its
abominable stringent cleanliness laws and observances.
King envisioned a world house which had been inherited
by humankind in which we have to live together—"black
and white, Easterner and Westerner, Gentile and Jew,
Catholic and Protestant, Moslem and Hindu—a family un-
duly separated in ideas, culture, and interest, who, because
we can never again live apart, must learn somehow to live
with each other in peace." [4]

King's architectonic vision was told in the parable of
two strangers who would one day discover each other and
set off an unending chain reaction. He saw a young boy

sitting on a stoop in front of a Harlem apartment house. The boy is the victim of poor living conditions and a fatherless home. He envisioned also a young girl sitting on the stoop of a rickety one-family house in Birmingham, Alabama. These two strangers, separated by over a thousand stretching miles, stand up, square their shoulders, and lift their eyes toward heaven. They join hands across the miles and take a step together, no longer strangers, but brother and sister in the cause.

As long as the inhabitants of our world-house remain strangers to one another, desperately searching for recognition, our widespread loneliness will persist. Blessings from God will remain undelivered; causes will remain unfought; needs will remain unfilled; loneliness, in its social and existential forms, will shadow our living. The first step, then, in the journey toward conquering loneliness begins with the discovery of the strangers around us.

2.

LONELINESS
and the
Discovery of Relationships

Reclaiming Identity

Our world is made up of an awesome assortment of methods, programs, computers, techniques, theories, and groups, and our worth and importance as individuals are frequently obscured by society's drive for efficiency and maximization of profit. It is often next to impossible to be treated as a person. The increased tendency toward regimentation creates a dehumanization in which we are treated more like commodities than as the individual people we are. And in many instances we seem no longer to be able to choose with whom we do business. Perhaps nowhere is this process more evident than in banking procedures. We, of course, have to contend with long lines and with tellers who disappear as soon as we reach the head of the line. But the frustration doesn't end there, for we are then required to procure identification which will enable the clerk and computer to verify who we are, and keep tab on what we do.

My colleague Peter Gomes, minister of Memorial Church in Harvard University, tells the story of one lady who challenged the regimentation of banking.[1] She was the widow of a professor who had taught at the Episcopal seminary in Cambridge, Massachusetts, and had been a resident of the city for many years. She was a long-time patron of the Harvard Trust Bank. On a particular day, the lady presented herself at the teller's window only to hear the annoyingly efficient question: "Do you have any identification?" Rev. Gomes reports that the lady "drew herself up to full stature" and replied, "Young woman, I have banked in this bank since before you were born. I know perfectly well who I am. Who, may I ask, are you?"

This rather amusing story underlines the truth that one's identity is a precious thing. To lose identity, in the biblical sense, is to lose life. One's name, in the Scriptures, was not separated from one's being. The process of naming was depicted as being a part of creation itself. Before the process of creation was finished, the animals were brought before Adam to be "named"—to be completed.

Unfortunately, those institutions which could affirm individuality appear to be diminishing in our society. Often the Christian churches become as regimented as secular institutions. The church sometimes operates as if the institution were more important than the individuals who compose it. Many ecclesiastical choices are made on the basis of "not failing" as a smooth operating institution. Expanded budgets, peer pressure for larger congregations, overbuilt facilities, and Protestant competitiveness cause many ministers to view human beings as plums to be picked or scalps to be taken in the upbuilding of the institution. Instead of a "sanctuary" from a calculating and mercenary secular world, Sunday's church often becomes an extension of weekday methods to achieve weekday ends. Pastor friends of mine have lamented the fact that their churches contain so many members that they cannot even call parishioners by name. Yet rising operating expenses and a mobile society demand an ever-increasing revolving-door approach to church life. One pastor told me that his large parish had to "take in" over five hundred new members a year to simply "break even." What a breath of fresh air it would be to find a community of genuine congeniality in the middle of the unmeaningful frenzy of life. Such a "find" could revitalize and rehumanize life.

Not long ago my wife and I were making what we thought would be a routine trip. Like everyone else who lives in the South and wants to travel by plane, we had to make a connection with another flight out of Atlanta, Georgia. As we calmly walked up to the departure gate, we became aware of an unusual bustle of activity. People were scurrying around with exasperated looks on their faces. Mothers with little children in tow were running down the corridor to other gates. The gate and waiting room area was in a state of bedlam and confusion, and we soon found why. A computer in Jacksonville, Florida, had broken down and a needed piece of radar equipment was not put on the jumbo jet that we were due to travel on. So the plane had turned back and our flight was delayed two hours. Flight plans were ruined and an airline executive was even having to make hotel reservations for people to spend the night in Atlanta and catch flights the next morning. The moods were as diverse as the people: panic, anger, anxiety.

I projected all three. Taking advice from a fellow passenger that maybe I could get another flight, I hurried to a flight information desk. The employee punched vital information into his computer. Sorry, nothing there. But if I ran down to another desk a quarter of a mile away, a gentleman had a tie-in to another computer and maybe it would turn up a flight. So the race was on. But in each instance the computer spilled out its bad news: nothing available!

So we were stuck. The computer in Jacksonville had blown it, the other computers could not help, and two hundred of us were in limbo. When we got back to the original gate, most of the people were sitting around talking. Exasperation had turned into stoic resignation. Everything had been tried, and we were stranded together for better or worse.

Our common misery seemed to bring us together in friendly conversation. People talked about themselves and their families. Pictures of children were passed around. A group began playing cards. The atmosphere changed from panicked frenzy to genuine congeniality, and small talk displaced our anger and consternation. I learned from a United States senator that his children like chocolate caramels better than any other form of candy. A gentleman in a wheelchair talked about the construction business in Virginia and gave me advice about the best way to get through Dallas during rush-hour traffic. I even learned a bit about exploratory stomach surgery from a fellow passenger.

What an amazing phenomenon—the computer blew and a group of people rediscovered the beauty of human relationships. It was as if we were all sitting in the eye of a hurricane. While the world raged about us, we were experiencing a lull. No one was afraid of what people would think if they spoke. No one feared being embarrassed or causing embarrassment to others. We just listened to the good that was in one another and tried to respond to it.

In thinking about that particular experience, I have become acutely aware of the drive to reclaim identity and affirm our humanity which links us with men and women of all time. Ralph Waldo Emerson's words, written over a century ago, put it well:

> How many persons we meet in houses, who we scarcely speak to, who yet we know, and who know us! How many we see in the street, or sit with in church, whom though silently, we warmly rejoice to be with! Read the language of these wandering eyebeams. The heart knoweth.
>
> *(Essays on Friendship,* 1841)

Reclaiming the Quality of Life

In many ways, that first Christmas was an eye in the center of a hurricane. As religious leaders jockeyed for prominent positions, merchants wheeled and dealed in the marketplace, and families remained loyal to old superstitions and prejudices, a child was born in Bethlehem. The child opened up the way to a new relationship with God. For many, life would change from frenzy into genuine congeniality. In the midst of bedlam and confusion, former strangers opened themselves to one another, attained a new identity (as children of God) , and discovered the quality of life. Tax collectors, lawyers, and fishermen began to question their passion for money and replaced it with a passion for relationships. A new kind of world was emerging, one which would emphasize the quality and not the quantity of life. Into a frenzied society came one who called people to rediscover the beauty and richness of relationships through healthy love of God, neighbor, and self.

Perhaps our greatest need is to rediscover relationships; our very existence depends upon them. So often we become so preoccupied with professional and familial fulfillment that we leave untapped the vast reservoir of human potential that is around us. Yet, loving intimacy—relating more meaningfully to our neighbors—is a far more essential ingredient to our future happiness and satisfaction than accumulating more of life's luxuries.

David Neiswanger of the Menninger Foundation says, "If each of us can be helped by science to live a hundred years, what will it profit us if our hates and fears, our loneliness and our remorse will not permit us to enjoy them?" [2]

How true that is! Happily, people today are beginning to concentrate on the quality of life rather than the quantity of life. After all, a hundred years of Coca-Cola, Dr. Pepper, Big Macs, television, parties, weddings, and new automobiles would not be a very exciting or fulfilling prospect in life. And I don't believe that a hundred years of prima donna preaching, inspiring choral anthems, denominational offices, stained glass windows, and collection plates full of dollars would be a very exciting or fulfilling prospect in the life of a church.

But if society or church is committed to people and causes that they believe in, the idea of living one hundred years takes on new meaning. It seems to me this is precisely what the church can and must give people—the rediscovery of relationships, causes, and health. In reading our New Testament we discover that loving intimacy, the primary of personal relationships, was a characteristic of the fellowship of the early church. The purpose of our written Gospels was to tell the good news about the discovery of this intimacy, not to present a historical document. Consequently, it seems contrary to the whole scheme of things for ministers and lay persons to shy away from opening themselves to one another and to strangers in our highly transient world. Why are we so fearful of revealing the most precious thing in our Christian heritage, our vulnerable personhoods?

The Risk in Relationship

I think the answer lies in that word "vulnerable." Jesus called people not to relate to one another in old ways and patterns but to open themselves up and risk new patterns of getting to know one another. Christ's people are called to live growingly, to structure flexible relationships. Either we grow and change or we die.

Perhaps the most poignant example of this is to be found in Jesus' example of the new wine and old wineskins. When wineskins were old and dried, they were more vulnerable to pressure from within. They easily formed cracks. And when new wine was poured into those old skins, Jesus predicted disastrous results because the still fermenting new wine would expand and bring pressure on the old, inflexible containers—then the skins would burst and both contents and containers would be lost.

Following this analogy, Jesus charged bluntly that a religious system like that of the Pharisees was so inflexible that it couldn't contain the fermentation of the new spirit. Similarly, at the personal level, inflexibility cannot contain the spiritual fermentation. We must grow, and when we attempt to share our fears and inadequacies, we begin to trust each other. And the more trust grows, the less important become our fears.

The church, says Reuel Howe, is supposed to be "a fellowship of vulnerable human beings sharing with each other in such a way that they grow a trust and a faith that opens them to each other and to the God in their midst." [3]

Reclaiming Our Cause

Early one morning a social worker friend of mine set out to make her routine visits among the elderly. She walked up the steps of a huge two-story frame house and knocked on the door. Not receiving a response, she pushed the door open and called the gentleman's name. When she received no answer, she stepped inside and started a check of each room. Upon entering a bedroom she found him slumped over a table. Empty whiskey bottles littered the floor.

She worked at bringing him around, and as stupor turned into sobriety, he poured out his pathetic story. He was alone in life. That bitter pain of loneliness had consumed his personality like a fire raging through dry timber. Each personal and social security check he received was immediately cashed and the money spent to produce another drunken stupor in a frantic effort to drown the loneliness.

After a time my friend asked me to help. The three of us were talking one day when the head of a charitable organization dropped by with a tale of woe about losing their janitor and not having enough funds to hire a new one. Suddenly the idea occurred to me that possibly the old gentleman would be interested in volunteering to help out, but it seemed a little touchy because he was one of the wealthiest persons in town. It was almost ludicrous to think that he would empty trash and do cleaning without pay, but we decided to ask him anyway.

Much to my amazement he consented eagerly, and he became a vital part of the organization as a volunteer janitor. Once or twice a week I'd drive by and see him working busily, and whenever I stopped to talk he would take over the conversation with stories about some project the organization was engaged in.

Now his routine is established, and he has a fresh purpose. Each morning he awakens, shaves, puts on his best vested suit, and walks over to the building to carry out the trash. The garbage cans are always washed. No litter is found on the property, and he no longer drinks. His new life came through having a cause to belong to, something greater than himself to which he could ascribe allegiance and work for.

A sense of worth and happiness comes through being needed, through giving ourselves to a cause. Each of us experiences this need. Without a cause, a purpose, we become lonely and drift through life. Sigmund Freud believed that loving and working are the two most effective ingredients of mental health. Both are essential if life is to become a pilgrimage and not a dreadful, lonely, and fatiguing grind. Paul Pruyser, a clinical psychologist in the Menninger Foundation, speaks of vocation as "putting one's talents to work as a participant in the process that moves the universe toward increasing integrity." [4]

The Corporate Imperative

Obedience to a cause greater than ourselves is the central idea of the life of Jesus, but, unfortunately, we tend to think of obedience as a negative or gloomy thing. Perhaps our minds call up images of past authority figures who would punish us if we were not obedient. Or perhaps we pick up on an insecure minister who insisted that Christianity was synonymous with our presence at church every time the door was open. But for Jesus and his followers, obedience to the cause was not regimented gloom or a burden; it was a satisfaction laced with joy.

I don't wish to imply here that the mechanics of church life should take precedence over family or personal lives or that we should exonerate those "purists" who get buried in the trappings and routines of religious experience and neglect their other responsibilities. Far from it! But I firmly believe that all of us need a cause higher than ourselves and, yes, on occasion even higher than our own families. We need a stake in something that is a part of the ebb and flow of history. We must find integration with the created order, with the whole of life, and not just with one of its segments. Friends and children grow up, move, and die. Society itself can blow hot and cold, becoming as mean as it is kind. But to remain whole, each of us must belong to a cause that incorporates *abiding* self-worth.

Amazingly enough, the most obvious symbols of achievement in life do not bring the deepest joy and most enduring feelings of self-worth. Enduring value comes through our caring deeply for others and in experiencing their caring for us. In Christian terminology, we speak of this as belonging to a caring Christian community, and, in my judgment, genuine self-worth is difficult to find outside of such a community where we learn to be accountable to others for our thoughts and actions. How else can we take the risks which right action demands unless we belong to a community where we can be persons, not roles, to one another? [5]

The story of Jesus riding into Jerusalem on that first Palm Sunday appeals to me because it points up the fact that Christianity is visible allegiance to a cause, the Kingdom of God. Salvation is not just a strictly personal thing; it has a corporate dimension. One of the most moving scenes in gospel history is that procession of disciples and the Christ moving into Jerusalem on Palm Sunday. The Kingdom of God was at hand. That triumphal entry overshadowed the day of distress, discouragement, and disbelief which had preceded that moment. Here was a cause to attach oneself to.

We Christians owe a great debt to a Baptist minister of the late 1800s and early 1900s for a refocusing of the corporate nature of Christianity. Walter Rauschenbusch graduated from Rochester Seminary in 1886 and was called to be the pastor of the Second German Church in New York City. That immigrant church was situated in the depressed urban slums of the city, and it was here that Rauschenbusch awoke to the problems of society. He recognized that a great gulf existed between a gospel suited only for the individual and one focused on the needs of the entire social system. His life's concern became the advancement of Christianity as a Kingdom concept. His unpublished work "The Righteousness of the Kingdom" emphasized Jesus as initiator of a cause:

> The Kingdom of God is the first and the most essential dogma of the Christian faith. It is also the lost social ideal of Christendom. No man is a Christian in the full sense of the original discipleship until he has made the Kingdom of God the controlling purpose of his life, and no man is intellectually prepared to understand Jesus Christ until he has understood the meaning of the Kingdom of God.[6]

Strict individualism is not the product of genuine Christian expression, and our world needs its proper focus on the corporate nature of Christianity. Jesus began in ministry with the words, "Repent, the Kingdom of God is at hand" (Matt. 4:17). As his ministry on earth drew to its conclusion, he entered Jerusalem publicly to claim the Kingdom and to confront the leaders of the nation with the claims of his cause.

To be sure, his was not the type of kingdom many people of that day expected. He was a new kind of king, bringing a new kind of cause. He rode on a humble donkey, not in a chariot. There were no spears in the hands of his followers, only palm leaves. There was no staccato drumbeat, just songs of praise and joy. Yet a cause was pushed into the public forefront, and to the New Testament writers continuity of the cause was very important.

The reality of this corporateness was revealed vividly to me in an experience I had with a friend. One of the most influential people in my life is a physician in South Carolina. In the years I have known him he has become a father figure to me. He provided free medical services, counsel, and support during the time I was his pastor. A few years ago a stroke left him paralyzed on one side of his body. For many days it appeared that he would not even live. The family and I checked his insurance policies and worked with his attorney to make certain that everything was in order. Then, slowly but surely his body began to respond. Regaining the use of his paralyzed leg was the first sign. Then his limp arm improved and could comfortably rest in a sling. Hours of lifting weights and squeezing tennis balls strengthened his body, and finally, after three years, he reached 100 percent capacity and returned to performing surgery.

You don't live with someone like that through a period of intense trial without becoming very close. Consequently, I found myself dreading a particular conversation I knew was inevitable. I sat in my automobile outside his office trying to summon enough courage to go in and tell him I was leaving to take a church in Texas. Finally, when I saw him I blurted out my news and tried to get hold of my feelings so as to remain in control of my "cool" during his response.

In a very genuine, yet profound way, he simply responded, "We must all be about doing the Kingdom's work. You belong to a cause and you must go where that cause needs serving and do what that cause demands. We belong to a cause that transcends our individual situations." His affirmation moved me deeply and enabled me to see that the cause of Christ is much larger than my Protestant individualism.

A Corporateness in Death

Shortly after arriving at my new church in Waco, Texas, I met a woman who was fighting a losing battle against cancer. Her spirit in the face of such a devastating foe was magnificent. It was an uplifting experience to be with her. I recall one occasion when I walked into her room and caught her in an agonizing moment. She lay in the fetal position barely holding onto life. But as we talked, she tried to radiate warmth. She mentioned the church and what it meant to her, but even while we were talking she slipped into a semiconscious state. A nurse entered the room and politely told me that it was time to leave, but, as I started to leave, the patient cried out, "Harold, Harold." Then when I didn't respond, her mind became confused and she pleaded, "David, David, come back." As medication and confusion muddled her mind, I heard her cry as I walked down the hall, "Harold, David, Brother Melton, Harold." It was as if someone had left a beautiful water-color painting out in the yard and it was being rained on. The colors were all mixing together, the distinctiveness was flowing into corporateness, the human spirit was leaping generations and space and time to claim the cause that it belonged to.

David and Brother Melton are names of ministers who preceded me in that church. As my dear dying friend moved to the end of her life, she reached out to those who had embraced her in a kind of communal celebration. And she died, not as an isolated individual succumbing to overwhelming medical odds, but as a participant in the ongoing Kingdom of God, at home in the eternal family of God. Her spirit claimed its cause and its corporate entity.

Loneliness and Emotional Health

Certain people seem to have a particular gift for expressing deep and moving experiences in a way that really grabs our attention, and we identify with them. I encountered such an attention-grabber in the writing of a man who suffered from an illness which probably causes more human suffering than any other single disease.

His name is Percy Knauth, and he has written a book about his life entitled *A Season in Hell.*[7] His life was being turned inside out—everything he saw was negative. Where there should have been joy, he felt only unending sadness. When he had every reason to bask in the glow of his past accomplishments as an overseas reporter and writer and editor for *Time, Life,* and *Sports Illustrated,* he felt worthless. His life, enriched by a lovely wife of twenty years and two beautiful children, appeared to be of little value.

Percy chronicled a war with his nerves that reached the depths of depression. As he moved through a series of psychiatrists, medications, and searches for personal integration, he began to fight that loss of meaning which had propelled him into this battle with his nerves. Slowly and triumphantly he emerged a whole person. And as I read about his agony and his triumph over it, I reflected upon my experiences as a minister with parishioners who had also wrestled with this disease which causes so much misery.

While few of us will reach such extreme depths of depression, our own sense of loneliness will in one way or another cause us to do battle with our nerves. There will be times when in depression or possibly even in frustration we may slip into the destructive feeling that we don't mean much to our family, our job, or even ourselves.

Society today has generated a plethora of help for our efforts to combat a host of perplexing maladies. We have created pamphlets, television commercials, and a constant run of advice to help us fight heart disease, cancer, tuberculosis, and sickle cell anemia. But little advice is offered on how to combat depression. And yet, Doctor Stanley Lesse in doing research on depression found that 50 percent or more of hospital patients ages 40 through 60 had variations of depression. Indeed, headaches, backaches, loss of appetite, upset stomach, insomnia, fatigue, and stiff neck are all symptoms which *may* be caused by depression.

Depression, in its many forms, has been fought, won, or lost, by persons since the beginning of history. Perhaps the first recorded incident of a depressive state is to be found in the Bible. The eighteenth chapter of 1 Samuel records that an "evil" spirit came upon King Saul. Apparently these moods came over Saul with some regularity, for Scripture states that this was not the first time a boy named David had been summoned to play music for the king. Saul attempted to lift his depression by having young David play his lyre and sing his psalms. And according to the story, this music therapy apparently gave some relief. The power of music therapy was impressed on me quite forcibly one Sunday when I decided that it would be adventuresome to alter the conclusion to our sacrament of communion. My usual course was to repeat Mark 14:26, "Then they sang a hymn and went out to the Mount Olives" (TEV) and have the congregation conclude the service by holding hands and singing a hymn. Instead, I eliminated the hymn and asked the congregation to depart in silence.

Following the service, a parishioner, visibly shaken, stopped by my office. The absence of the traditional hymn had produced a vacuum in his worship experience and he told me why. It seems that an alcoholic father, a war in Vietnam which he had fought in but not understood, and a soured love affair had produced a serious mental de-

pression in his life. In fact, he had spent time in a nearby
psychiatric hospital several years before. At that time his
psychiatrist, knowing of the patient's lifetime love for
music, prescribed a form of music therapy as a means of
combating the depression. Further conversation with my
friend that day helped me see that the singing of a traditional hymn following our communion service actually had
a therapeutic affect on him, and when it was omitted, he
felt threatened and disturbed. Knowing this, and understanding better my friend's problems enabled me to be of
greater help and support in his fight against depression.

I relate this story because it serves as an example of how
we who plan and lead worship in any setting are sometimes
oblivious to the personal wars that individuals are fighting
with their own nerves and how worship must arise out of
those shared and felt human struggles. Indeed, we in the
church can preach and teach of Jesus on Sunday, pat one
another on the back in glowing convivialities, and utter
pious platitudes, but on Monday through Saturday we're
rubbing shoulders in the day-to-day routines of life with
loved ones and friends who are hurting badly. Some may
be fed up with two much drinking and superficial social
exchanges. Others may be struggling with a budget which
will not stretch far enough. Still others may be involved with
a host of crippling personal and vocational crises.

It seems to me that coping with these kinds of problems
should be a major goal for our preaching, worship, teaching, and gathering in a Christian community—helping one
another to meet the pressures and circumstances of life
which cannot be readily changed. And, having said this,
let's examine certain things we need to remember and consider as we attempt to overcome, and help others to overcome, the crippling effects of depression.

Perhaps the single most important contribution we and

*the church can make to human health is to accept the idea
that a personal problem is not necessarily a sign of lack of
faith.* Other than communicating the love of God, I sincerely believe that an acceptance of this truth is the para-
mount need within a positive Christian community.

Unfortunately, Christians have often had trouble ad-
mitting and conquering emotional crises. There is a tendency to refuse to admit depression, moodswing, and other
byproducts of the wavering emotions because we have considered these to be signs of a lack of faith. Now, I believe
that God created men and women with nerves and emotions.
These are a part of being human, and Christianity is a *response* to human life, not a denial of it. Such being the case
I think it will be helpful to take a brief look at some of the
workings of our emotions and nerves.

The brain is a marvelous control center which receives
signals and sends our responses. If we prick our skin with a
pin, a signal is sent to the brain and the response goes back,
"Stay away from the point of the pin." The process happens
so quickly that we are not immediately aware of it, and if
something delays or distorts the circuit, the process may
not take place at all. For example, novocaine can deaden
nerve fibers to the point that the signal goes to brain cells
faintly or not at all. A needle or knife can then probe our
skin and no response is sent from the brain to the area. Obviously, this makes visits to the dentist's office a little more
pleasant.

On the other hand, some of the signals received by the
brain have to do with moods or emotions. A joyful event
sends a signal to the brain and a delightful response is produced. A threatening event sends a signal of fear to the brain
and we become tense and alert. For every mood there is a
signal and an appropriate response. But again something
can alter that circuit. The nerve fibers can become dead-

ened. Certain events and pressures can, like novocaine, override the normal emotional response, and persons can become depressed when they should be joyful.

Most of the time this overriding process is a healthy one. Periods of feeling "blue" or "let-down" after intense excitement serve a useful purpose. They slow us down, and enable our body forces to mobilize again. A depressed period retards our heartbeat and lowers our blood pressure, enabling us to lick our emotional wounds. But sometimes the circuit remains overridden. We fall into despair and lose self-esteem and start to feel worthless.

The amazing thing about prolonged depression is that at its basic level *it is really repressed anger*. It is a masked cry for love and attention. We all need recognition and assurance that we are appreciated and valuable. We need stroking from other people. Unfortunately, though, we seldom ask for attention and love because we don't think we should. Consequently, those emotional needs are repressed. We wouldn't think of standing up in a church or group setting and saying, "Tell me I am worth something. Please recognize me and tell me that I am loved." We seldom claim love in that manner. But we must claim it somehow, so we do it through the cry of sadness or playing the games of "poor me" and "ain't it awful." We hope that eventually someone will tell us how good we are and give us the stroking we need for affirmation. Yes, our emotions are often numbed or overridden by the *anger* we feel at not being loved, and our entire system can unconsciously become paralyzed by the anger we feel when we think others aren't paying enough attention to us.

I sincerely believe that Jesus understood this make-up of human personality as well as anyone has. The essence of his preaching and teaching was geared toward affirmation and fulfillment, something he called "the abundant life." He not only recognized the way men and women function; he gave some practical handles to help us through the war of nerves and depression.

In the first place, Jesus emphasized self-analysis instead of looking for others to blame as a step toward healthy-mindedness. I'm amazed at the psychological health which characterized the life-style of Jesus. Whenever a major decision or event confronted him, he withdrew to a quiet place. Once in the frantic efforts of a large crowd to reach him, he got in a boat and withdrew from them. It seems to me that regular self-examination was a part of his routine. When he gave the example of the publican and the sinner praying, Jesus praised not the one who focused on other people but the one who went to a private place and looked at himself before God. This will help us not to overreact to circumstances.

Another way to combat depression and nervous exhaustion is to hand oneself some little triumphs. This helps us to concentrate on what we do well. Our sense of competitiveness, often good for the business world, becomes a liability in the personal sphere. When we insist on comparing our weaknesses with another's strengths, destructive and crippling patterns ensue. One way to counteract this is with what I call a "success" chart. Here is how it works. First, a list is made of the talents a person believes he or she has which contribute toward the greatest vocational and personal success. Then the person is asked to list areas of life which hold the least possibility of success. Finally, an outside friend is asked to develop a similar chart for the person from his or her perspective. As can be imagined, in many cases, perceptions of strengths and weaknesses differ sharply, and it is quite revealing to compare the results. As a rule, the observer-friend will help the depressed person to see in a new and fresh way strengths and abilities which had been long suppressed or completely forgotten.

For some, a success chart plainly shows the need to change situations which are not productive. We hear, I think, some good words of advice from Jesus to his disciples: ". . . wherever they do not receive you, when you leave that town shake off the dust from your feet as a testimony against them" (Luke 9: 5). We are not going to be successful in everything, and Jesus apparently places no virtue in masochistic yearnings nor in wasting time and emotional energy in an unreceptive situation. Given our need for experiencing some little triumphs and affirmations in life, I believe that one of the cardinal virtues of church life is its ability as a volunteer institution to enable people who perform meaningless, even thankless, tasks in secular society to attain well-deserved positions of leadership and self-affirmation. Where else can, as I have seen in several churches, a garbage collector become the leading figure in the committee structure of an institution, a 90-year-old woman become a revered teacher of children, and a one-armed house painter have a building named after him for years of devotion and service in directing a building and grounds committee? All of this simply points up the need for the church to be the place where little triumphs may be achieved by people as they attempt to use their varying abilities in the service of the Lord.

Perhaps one of the most effective means of overcoming depression and negative buried feelings is to have intimate friends to whom we can express ourselves without fear of reprisal. Jeremiah cursed God on more than one occasion and let his secretary, Baruch, know just how he felt about the way things were going. Elijah angrily shouted out at God numerous times. Jesus on more than one occasion spoke of his enemies as "fools," and he referred to the Pharisees as a "brood of vipers."

I believe this strong ventilation of feelings is essential to emotional health and that it doesn't indicate a lack of faith. One of the first things psychiatrists do with chronically depressed people is try to get them in comfortable individual or group settings where they can ventilate their true feelings.

Often we have viewed the church fights, criticisms, and angry denunciations within the Christian community as signs of weakness. In many instances this is correct. But properly understood and managed, even the ventilations of feelings which take place there can have redemptive qualities and be a sure sign of health. Self-analysis, positive affirmation of the good that we do, and ventilation of feelings within the love of a positive Christian community can lead to a fresh discovery of emotional health.

Loneliness, Family, and Support Systems

There is an intriguing legend about the pipe which Moses played when he gathered Jethro's sheep on the hillside of Midian. Legend has it that the pipe was found centuries after the death of Moses, and as the years passed, came to be recognized as a religious relic. But as the crowds clamored to view the pipe, someone decided that it was just too ordinary-looking to be associated with someone as majestic as Moses. After much consultation, they decided to overlay the crude pipe with pure gold. It was now beautifully ornate but utterly useless because it couldn't be played; its clear note was ruined and its usefulness as a musical instrument was lost forever.

I see this story as analogous with the situation of today's family. I would like to remove some of the "ornateness" laid upon family roles and in simple, positive terms point out and illustrate how parents and children can be useful to one another in the attempt to support each other in the battle against loneliness and for meaning. Unfortunately, we have loaded the family relationship with so many ornate trappings that its true function as a loving, redemptive community is lost entirely.

Parents and children, of course, can come together to develop a system of tremendous personal support and affirmation to shield against many of the hurts in life. Irving Janis calls such a system "emotional inoculation." [8] An emotional inoculation system provides a person with realistic information about what might be coming in life, reassures the person that he or she can survive stress, and provides help in finding means of self-protection.

In writing the second letter to Timothy the Apostle Paul offered encouragement by reminding him of the emotional support system he had inherited through his mother and grandmother. Paul encouraged Timothy to tap the emotional reservoir which had been passed along to him through three generations.

For the thoughtful person, there can be no question about the importance of the parental image in our personal faith development. The most significant biblical images of God revolve around the parenting relationship. Isaiah compared God's love with that of a mother (49:15; 66:13). Jesus longed to protect Jerusalem's children as a mother hen gathers her chicks under her wings (Luke 13: 34). And we are all familiar with the image of heaven implied in Jesus' parable about a prodigal son who returns to his father.

Being a parent is no easy job. Many kinds of change are involved especially when separation occurs. When a child leaves home for college, or for anywhere else, separation frequently means painful change. Those shifting relationships seem to parallel, in a sense, the ventures taken in exploring space. In essence, a college student also is exploring space—educational, psychological, and emotional space—and to do that he or she must pull away from the gravity of home for a time.

Join with me for a moment in picturing the make-up of the launching of major space ventures by NASA. The special bulletins which intermittently interrupt regular television viewing give accounts of control shifting from one state to another. As a rocket blasts off in its bid to escape the gravitational pull of the earth, a tremendous force is needed. Great quantities of fuel and energy are needed to thrust that ship out of earth's atmosphere into the freedom of outer space. As the craft reaches that stage of freedom, the crucial factor shifts from the thrust power to the life-support systems. Here things get complicated. Whereas it took *one* extremely powerful system to hurl the craft into freedom, it now takes *hundreds* of computerized systems to keep the persons inside the craft healthy and alert.

I see a striking parallel here with family influences on children. When they are growing through childhood and adolescence, it takes a tremendous force from parents to assemble the necessary monetary, emotional, moral, religious, intellectual, and physical fuels for the youth to be lifted toward freedom to explore the world. But once the young person is on his or her way beyond the gravity of home, the family becomes but a part of the complex life-support system. Regardless of camaraderie, love, and frequent visits, once we leave home, we can never totally go back to our parents again.

In trying to understand and catch the spirit of how Jesus encouraged and challenged people around him to move toward a healthy and fulfilled life, it seems clear that he always affirmed the primary place of the family as the warm

and loving center of support for each member—yet he did
not expect his followers to center all their political and religious emotions in the family.

What a difficult yet essential shift that is: from total
thrust to but a part, admittedly a major one, of a host of
support systems. It demands not only compromise and
negotiation on the part of parents but on the part of the
child as well. After all, a student away from home cannot
legitimately expect his family to continue to be the center
of his religious, political, and emotional needs.

For example, in the total life-support systems of an astro-
naut, a computerized system dispenses his food. Were he
to expect that same system to provide him with recreation,
reading materials, oxygen, and vital flight information, his
health would be in danger. His overloading of the system
would be a refusal to use something wonderful in the
proper way.

Let's face it, parents' political views are not *always* the
same as their children's, and it isn't likely they are reading
the same books or are involved in the same recreational activities. The old home church may not mean the same thing
to the young person as to the parent, but none of these
things should produce anxiety. We need to remember that
as parents our job was to help launch our children into their
inner and outer space, but when that has been accomplished, we should back off, recognizing that our total thrust
responsibility has been accomplished.

What then does the family do? What is the place it oc-
cupies among those systems necessary to support life? I
know of no better way to put it than to say that the family
can and should become *the emotional inoculation system.*
That is the pivotal element in any support system. While
no one can go home again, the fact remains that home is
where we first discovered that in the midst of all the terror

and nothingness of life we are loved. In addition, the family remains the one place people rely on to cushion themselves from the disappointments, failings, and hurts in life.

A pivotal resource in my own pilgrimage was reading the autobiography of the great scientist Charles Darwin.[9] History records Charles Darwin as a world-shaker, and he was. His *The Origin of Species* (1859) gave birth to a theory of evolution that shook the foundations of science and religion. The shock-waves have not yet receded over a hundred years later. And his work, *The Descent of Man,* written in 1871, helped establish him as a major figure in world history. Charles Darwin has influenced our lives as much as perhaps any human being could.

But his autobiography is most revealing. He wrote that as a schoolboy and a young man he took intense delight in historical plays, poetry, and music. But, then, things took a drastic turn and he wrote about it in these piercing words:

> Now for many years I cannot endure to read a line of poetry: I have tried . . . and found it so intolerably dull that it nauseated me. I have also lost almost any taste for pictures or music. . . . My mind seems to have become a kind of machine for grinding out general laws out of large collections of fact, but why this should have caused the atrophy of that part of the brain alone, on which the higher tastes depend, I cannot conceive. . . . The loss of these tastes is a loss of happiness, and may possibly be injurious to the intellect, and more probably to the moral character by enfeebling the emotional part of our nature.[10]

Those are tragic but true words. If the emotional part of our nature is enfeebled, the end result is loss of happiness. But, fortunately, in the Scriptures and human history we are presented vivid illustrations of the other side of the coin. In fact, the whole history of the New Testament is that of emotional inoculations from one generation to another, of rekindled gifts of God.

The converse to Darwin's attitude came for me in the life of my faculty adviser in seminary, George Ernest Wright, president of the American School of Oriental Research, curator of one of the world's greatest Semitic museums, and a world-shaker in the fields of religion and archeology. But rolled into that personality were traits of midwestern farmer, friend of the church, and loving parent. As we were discussing my academic schedule one day, he told me a story about one of his relatives—a young man the rest of the family had disowned. George Ernest insisted that the parents and relatives on one side of the family were making a mistake: "A person can't live without his parents, and parents can't live without their children. You cannot enfeeble your emotions and systems of support and retain happiness." It was then that I grasped at the emotional level for the first time the significance of the biblical image of God as parent.

Life holds out for us its rewards and potentialities as well as its traumas and defeats. Whether we find the treasure of relationships through planned search or stumble across it quite unawares, it is there. A crucial step in conquering the loneliness that impinges upon us is the discovery of relationships. Without relationships there can be no community. Without community there can be no solidarity with our fellow men and women and with our God.

3.

LONELINESS
and the
Discovery of Community

The Advantage of Community

Sports fans are aware of the terminology "home court advantage." It means the advantage gained over an opponent through the presence of partisan fans and familiarity with the environment. Teams that are clearly physically inferior to an opponent will occasionally defeat that opponent through the psychological lift that comes from the cheers of the home crowd. On a neutral court the stronger team would easily dominate the game.

Even at the risk of sounding trite, I believe it is valid to call loneliness an opponent in life's pilgrimage. In the face of those forces which would rob us of meaningful activity and relationships, the presence of community becomes a necessity. Without the abundance of shared experiences and symbols, we never experience the security of caring and being cared for by brothers and sisters in the walk from our birth to our grave. Without others to share fear with us, stand by us in solidarity, and create the security of group rewards, we operate at a tremendous disadvantage in our efforts to conquer loneliness. The founders of our religion have long recognized the potency of community. In fact, the word *religion* itself is taken from the Latin word *religare*, meaning "to bind together."

All of us operate among two great influences in life: the constitutional factors in our personality and the cultural factors around us. There is very little we can do to change the constitutional factors around us. There is very little we can do to change the constitutional factors we have inherited. We may wish that we were blessed with our grandmother's brains instead of her big nose, or with our father's curly hair instead of his irregular teeth. The degree of intelligence, artistic sensitivity, and body build we have inherited are part of our "givens" in life. But the cultural factors are entirely within our powers of discernment and initiative. They can nurture or enfeeble our emotional and spiritual growth. Not the least of these is a community of faith.

It seems to me there is a great lack of understanding today concerning what is actually involved in the process of conquering loneliness through participation in a Christian community. Some fall prey to the exhibitionism of quasi-revivalistic efforts, and others leave family, home, and friends to become part of the rapidly expanding phenomena of religious cults in the United States. Many people have a difficult time because they have developed utopian goals and in their pain of loneliness have projected those goals onto the Christian church. The dynamics of the Christian community are complicated and our lonely world needs to discover not only their complexity but their promise as well.

A Human Institution and Its Imperfections

Most disillusionments with God and feelings of anger, frustration, and even revenge toward the community of the gathered people of God, which we call the "church," stem from the basic realization that the church is a human community, filled with imperfections.

For some of us this disillusionment took place in adolescence. Our drive for acceptance, mingled with genuine religious inquiry, placed us in church only to discover that the awesome loneliness or loss of *anticipated* meaning overwhelmed us. Perhaps we created a hero out of some Sunday school teacher and later found out that the hero had clay feet. Perhaps we envisioned a church as a place for saints and discovered certain things about the members' lives which were far removed from sainthood. Adolescent reactions to such disillusionment have taken the form of rebellion, truancy, and, at times, even spin-offs into high school and college nonchurch religious groups and Bible studies that frequently claim to be "purer" than the church. We understand such reactions and cope with them. And eventually large numbers of these young people grow in their faith development and learn to adjust to the church as a *human* institution. Many even grow to celebrate it and lead the church to new heights. They give us new meanings and forms with which to combat the fact of personal and societal loneliness.

But more and more people today are having their initial encounter with the crucial loneliness problem in adulthood. Many are discovering that the church is an intensely human organization. They find that their utopian dreams of Christian community where everybody loves one another and gets along together all of the time will never be realized. Driven into the search for religious experience by the tremendous impact of loneliness, they are really visualizing a false form of community relationships without an adequate understanding of the fact that Christianity possesses a type of communal expression uniquely its own. They have little understanding to reflect upon and fall prey to those who can offer easy answers and a regimented lifestyle replete with utopian rhetoric. Their brush with church disappoints them. Church does not become an extension of their own egos, a confirmation of their partial view of reality. Not all relationships are found to be comfortably supportive. Church means collision of egos and the pain of not always getting one's way. Consequently, we are finding more and more adults disillusioned, apathetic, or angry toward the church. They cast around for those groups which on the surface appear to be less jaded by the human element.

This problem in our lonely world demands that we stake our perimeters of Christian community and offer its contribution to the loneliness problem. What do we offer that the other world religions do not? How can we understand ourselves in a world so desperate for community that over 900 lonely people are willing to turn over their entire assets and ultimately their lives to a cult leader who held out Guyana as the promised land? How can our human witness with all of its imperfections appeal to a fragmented, lonely world?

One of the distinctive claims of Christian community is precisely at the point of its humanity. Other world religions promise a community free of weakness, full of prayer and inward meditation, and a march toward perfection. Buddhism and Zen, Hare Krishna, and some of the inward Oriental movements in our country, even our Protestantism, have *ends* of *Christian* community. Our Scriptures and church history remind us that Christian community never has been nor will be a flourishing utopian garden. Instead, Christian community has been a place of promise, struggle, and discipline where God prepares parched earth for the planting of the Kingdom. Likeness and absence of conflict are not a part of Christian community. *Church is a human community guided by God, and not a divine community guided by humans.* That defi-

nition distinguishes authentic Christianity from counter-
feits. When I encounter individuals who earnestly desire a
community totally oriented around introspection, meditation, and in-group awareness, I wish that they would use
another name for their persuasion instead of *Christianity*.

Most of the Bible was written to affirm the church as a
human community, full of weaknesses, guided by God. The
first readers of the Gospels were Christian. They were familiar with Jesus and with most of the main events in his
life. Many of his sayings were known to them through their
teachers and preachers. Why, then, were the Gospels written?

The Gospel of Mark was written to the church in Rome
which had just passed through fierce persecution at the
hands of Nero in A.D. 64. That congregation had been put
to a severe test. Both Peter and Paul are believed to have
laid down their lives in this persecution. The temptation to
deny the Christian faith must have been in the hearts of
many Roman Christians. The words of Mark 13: 12 that
"brother will deliver up brother to death" were very real to
those people. Imagine their disillusionment with Christianity. They thought they had been brought into a utopian,
loving community of soul brothers and soul sisters. Then
for the first time they saw what was below the surface. Instead of strong souls, they discovered weakness, and instead
of a divine community, they found a human one. Just
imagine how utterly disillusioned they must have been!

Knowing that these were the people to whom the first
Gospel was written, we can understand, then, why it was
not written from a dry, orderly point of view. Even such
important characters as the disciples are introduced without the customary background information. And, in comparison with other accounts, far more care and space is given
to the trial and death of Jesus than might be expected. Un-

usual emphasis seems to be given to the failure Jesus experienced with Judas, the lethargy of the disciples in Geth-
semane, the denials of Peter, and even the questionings of
Thomas.

What an impact that Gospel of Mark must have had on
those early Christians! Peter was a beloved figure in their
recent memory, and the fact that even with all of his
strength—even in the early days—he had denied his Lord
must have encouraged them in their weakness. Yes, the
Gospel fell with great impact upon those whose utopian
dreams of church were falling apart in the face of human
weakness, for here was a running account which assured
them they were not alone in their struggle.

The element of human weakness is unmistakably por-
trayed in the life, death, and resurrection of Jesus. As we
lonely people in a dehumanizing and impersonal society
attempt to overcome our particular loneliness through
search for a religious community, it is important for us to
understand on a feeling level that our Christian fellowship
began and continued as a human institution. And if we can
acknowledge our personal loneliness and the presence of
human imperfection in the Christian community, we will
begin to read and understand the gospel message with au-
thenticity. Instead of trying to buy our community in
utopian weekend chunks in human potential centers, we
should be joining with other weak, fallible human beings
who come together under a vision and a faith stronger than
themselves and in the name of Christ step forward to heal
some hurt, right some wrong, and give some service. Then
we will begin to discover that even our imperfections are
aided and pulled along by the living God, and our fellow
strangers and neighbors will become brothers and sisters.
Here is an important truth: loneliness becomes dissolved
through a supportive network of humans.

Toward Discernment

One September not long ago I realized that if we were to enjoy our fireplace during the cold winter months I had better get busy with the routine job of laying in kindling and firewood. In previous years we always gathered pine cones and twigs for kindling, and then some friendly landowner usually earmarked a couple of trees which we could cut down for the larger wood. This always involved a lot of backbreaking work.

The more I thought about the time and energy involved, the less enthusiastic I became with the project. I decided that it was time for a change, so I went to the store and purchased a supply of the imitation logs. Each log was labeled, "The Romance without the Heartache." That's what I wanted, and I knew the logs worked because I had seen them burning in the homes of some of our friends.

After enjoying several of the manufactured logs, I just happened one day to read the fine print on the wrapper: "Warning, do not break these logs. Highly pressed matter is extremely combustible when exposed to air." Several of my friends had also warned me against breaking the logs. Because of a peculiar twist in my nature, curiosity overcame caution and I grabbed an iron poker one night and smashed one of the logs while it was burning. I'll not soon forget what happened. The flames leaped out on the rug. As I tried to stomp them out, the pieces broke into more pieces and the flames spread. Finally I managed to pour enough water on the pieces of manufactured log to put out the fire. I learned my lesson: "Romance without the heartache" is indeed beautiful, but don't ever break that romance or you're in trouble!

I tell this story because the loneliness experience in our world has created an almost irrational pursuit of *instant* community, *instant* religion, and even *instant* Jesus. We see Christianity pressed and rolled into beautiful colors. Media campaigns and emotional appeals join movie stars and "born again" claimants in advocating a quick, striking, warm glow of religious sensitivity. But once that manufactured product breaks under the normal strains and imperfections of life, tragic confusion and despair can result. It takes time and energy to build a solid faith and a supportive Christian community. There aren't shortcuts and the imitations don't satisfy.

It seems to me that in many instances religious display can become a symptom instead of a cure for loneliness. It hides the deeper recesses of lonely spirits. This, in part, helps to explain the tremendous incongruities in today's world. One of the most religiously saturated periods in our history, the 1970s, has also witnessed the highest divorce rates. More Bibles and religious books are sold in America than ever before, but pornography is also selling at a record rate. Amazingly, one of the most religious generations in the history of America, in terms of acknowledgment of belief in God, also appears to be the most decadent generation.

In my opinion such decadence stems from a lack of understanding of our heritage as Christian community. Our pursuit of the instant has left us without the clear identity we need to build the type of supportive community that can liberate us from the shackles of loneliness. We are finding our "easy answers" less than satisfactory, and our paralysis neutralizes our talk about God. In fact, much "God talk" itself is precipitated by lack of community identity. We struggle to discern our roots as the people of God in our place, and authentic preaching gives way to mere talk *about* God.

H. H. Farmer, in his classic on preaching, *The Servant of*

the Word, contended that the "act of preaching is part of a larger system of personal relationships and cannot be rightly understood in separation from it. The preacher, his sermon, and his hearers are embedded in this larger system, and what the preaching effects largely depends upon it."

A community with no real sense of mission can neutralize what might otherwise be good preaching. Indeed, no minister in a virtuoso solo performance can give *instant* Christianity. The responsibility for proclamation is vested in the community identity.

So, conquering loneliness through community proclamation and support demands possession of the power of *discernment.* The Book of Hebrews maintains that ". . . the mature . . . have their faculties trained by practice to distinguish good from evil" (5: 14). Without the power of discernment, our loneliness controls us and we become drifting creatures on the uncertain winds of change and personal whim. Consequently, a major task of Christian community and individual pursuit of it is not entertainment in the name of Jesus, but the cultivation of a mature, discerning faith. This cultivation comes not through participation in an unfocused community but in one with a rather clear prophetic identity.

The Prophetic Imperative of Community

Jesus identified with the prophetic office. That identity ran all through his life. Consequently, the New Testament is an ethical as well as a personal statement, and the communities of faith are both inwardly and outwardly directed. Their symbol is not a blindfolded lady holding some scales that are equally balanced on either side. Balance is not the justice of God. *The symbol of the biblical witness is a*

*wild-eyed prophet holding scales in his hand with his
finger pressed down hard, on the side of the poor, the wid-
owed, and the oppressed.*

Our efforts to conquer loneliness need not be misguided
or nonfocused. As Christians we are supposed to integrate
our lives around both belief and service. Personal fulfillment through attachment to a public is not the kind of
service-oriented community-building envisioned by Christ.
As we attempt to conquer our personal loneliness without
being willing to become involved in helping others conquer
their loneliness, we will never fulfill the desired goal of
service in life. Loneliness need not obliterate our moral
decisiveness.

The scriptural account in John 5 of Jesus healing a man
by the pool of Bethesda is most significant for us in understanding Jesus' combination of prophecy and healing. In
the ancient world, superstition played a major role in religion and life. Every tree, every river, every stream, every
hill had its spirit. Xerxes, the Persian king, had his ma-
gicians sacrifice white horses and perform ceremonies each
time he crossed a stream. This was to appease the spirit that
lived there. This same kind of superstition was prevalent
in Jesus' day. In Jerusalem there was a pool fed by inter-
mittent springs. It was believed that an angel disturbed the
waters and whoever could get there first when that happened would be healed. Consequently, five porches were
built around the pool so that people suffering from any kind
of disease or disability could wait there for the water to
move.

Jesus happened to stop by that place on a certain Jewish
holiday. It was a rather strange place to find the Son of God.
While everyone else attended celebrations and parties, Jesus
wanted to be around people who were in need. He went to

a crippled man who had been looking for help for thirty-eight years. All during this time he had been living with pain, but every time the waters began to move and churn, someone would always beat him to the pool.

Then along came Jesus, and he refuted all the magic of Bethesda. With a face reflecting love and compassion, Jesus looked at this wreck of a man and asked, "Do you want to be healed?" And then moments later Jesus spoke the words that completely healed the man and made him whole. What a contrast to the so-called miracles at Bethesda! They were *enigmatic*—strange—an angel disturbing the water. They were *occasional*—only at certain times. They were *limited* to those who could get there first. They were *unavailable* to many people. In one powerful action Jesus refuted occasional, strange, limited, and unavailable miracles. He opened up a new power to people who had been indiscriminately grabbing at every religious stirring of the waters.

Now, you would think this dramatic healing of the crippled man would have made the religious leaders happy. It didn't, because they were threatened. *As long as the people remained ignorant, superstitious, and immature in their faith, the religious leaders could attract huge crowds.* This action of Jesus upset all their efforts at keeping people enslaved to their religious manipulations, so they trumped up a phony charge against the healed man for working on the Sabbath by carrying his bed off the porch. They were hoping this would discredit Jesus with the people.

Their efforts were in vain, because Jesus represented a breakthrough for human liberation. He refused to turn his gifts of healing in on themselves. He turned them in outward servanthood to the world. Jesus refuted the inward orientation of that society's "miracles" and created islands

of both healing and freedom in that society's experience
with him. His spiritual dynamism was not wasted in enigmatic, inward-looking expectations of healing.

Perhaps more than anyone before him or since, Jesus, as
God's representative, balanced inner spiritual healing with
the motivation to liberate the healed for action, thereby
transforming the myths that had been the exclusive pre-
rogatives of only a select few.

This prophetic imperative expresses itself in a sharing of
words, emotions, and actions in a fellowship of mutual love.
Sometimes I have found that incidents in ministry impinge
upon me in such a way as to force me to sacrifice public performance for private action.

One day a mother of four children slouched into my office.
Her face was haggard and drawn; the stoop in her shoulders
reflected tragic discouragement. She poured out a tale of
easy credit, unpaid bills, and of being deserted by her husband. Her children hadn't had new clothes for a couple of
years. It was obvious, too, that her self-esteem had collapsed
completely. She was down for the count and could see no
hope out ahead.

As we talked, I learned that at one time she had possessed
secretarial skills. After a telephone call to a business
friend, it was agreed that if she could qualify he was willing
to hire her, but she would have to take a typing test. Since
she didn't own a typewriter, she asked permission to practice on the one in the church office. We agreed and she and
three of her children took over an office next to mine while
I attempted to complete work on a sermon for the next
Sunday. But it wasn't long before the clatter of the typewriter and the shouts of the children so distracted me that
I couldn't make any sense out of what I was doing. Before
me on the desk lay the Bible, two theology books, several
magazines, and copious notes on yellow pads, but nothing

helped. Then, out of the depths of my frustration and irri-
tation a question flashed across my mind: what was most
important—helping one woman at that noisy typewriter or
finishing and polishing a sermon that I hoped would speak
to several hundred people on Sunday morning? Quite
honestly, my scale of values at that moment favored the
several hundred at orderly worship over the confusion in
the next room.

That question of priorities plagues most of us. As our own
needs and the needs of those around us seem to grow larger,
the temptation to retreat into an orderly structure becomes
so strong that we fail to participate in the loneliness experiences of people we are jostling with and against in our
homes, in stores, on the streets, in offices, and in church.

But I found some degree of comfort that day in my office
when I again reaffirmed my belief that the Christian witness is grounded in personal allegiance to the prophetic
imperative. Without personal experience our efforts at
corporate activities, especially worship, are hollow. Rhetoric without a similar level of experience is an empty and
hollow exercise. In some ways, really, worship can become
an exercise in loneliness—a regimented performance in
which purposeful activity and meaningful relationships are
lacking.

Much of the prophetic witness in the Scriptures concentrated on the loneliness of worship. Mere identification with
a community of faith was no guarantee of conquering the
awful estrangement between men and women and God.
Amos, Micah, Hosea, Jeremiah, Isaiah, and Jesus labored
to help their listeners see that *God is far more concerned
with right relations between men and women than with
scrupulous regard for public worship.*

The first chapter of Isaiah depicts God as viewing worship
without character as a burden he was tired of carrying. In

effect Isaiah was saying: "All your worship services, solemn
meetings, are driving me crazy." Amos referred to the songs
and melodies of worship as "noise" to which God would not
listen. In fact, throughout the prophetic books of our Bible
we bump up against the recurring theme that no splendor
of worship could offset a disregard for the moral demands
of God in social relationships.

I firmly believe this idea needs to rattle and shake our
thinking in the church now. We have spent so much time
and energy focusing on the loneliness of people outside the
church, implying that membership in a community of faith
will solve the loneliness problem. And in some cases this
will happen, but all too often our churches and their worship resemble David Reismann's "lonely crowd," Sören
Kierkegaard's "public," or T. S. Eliot's "hollow men." If
this is true, and I happen to believe it is, then people outside the church will only see a "lonely crowd" and "hollow
people." Computer science has coined a word expressive of
this phenomenon—"gigo." It is short for "garbage in, garbage out." No matter how marvelous the computer, if you
put garbage into it, you'll get garbage out. In similar vein
I speak of "lilo"—loneliness in, loneliness out. If there is
a cold atmosphere of loneliness in the church, no help can
be offered to ease the loneliness of those outside the church.
The Old Testament prophets hurled *their* moral charges at
the *members* of the religious organizations, and Jesus continued with the same theme. He concerned himself with
the behavior of those on the inside—his followers. And he
criticized them for seeing the speck in someone else's eye
while ignoring the plank in their own. He told them that
they were in danger of condemnation if they did not feed
the hungry, clothe the naked, and visit the sick and im-
prisoned. Jesus focused attention away from the world and
put it on his followers. He took the concept of witness in

Isaiah and built upon it. He knew that a testimony of a life decently lived makes more of a witness than anything else. Ortega y Gasset, a great philosopher, observed that "people do not live together merely to be together. They live together to do something together."

Our awarenesses have changed much in the past century. Every age has certain key words which distinguish it. The nineteenth century, for example, was an age of optimism. Words like "change," "progress," "freedom," and "individual" characterized thought. There was confidence in the frontier. It was thought that happiness and truth were simply lying dormant in humankind. Mark Twain studied American thought in *Huckleberry Finn*. He presented a matchless picture of a child of nature revolting against the tyrannies of family and village. The revolt was not an apprehensive one, full of insecurity, but a rather joyous liberation from the prejudices and conventions of old morality.

The complexities of twentieth-century life and the decline of credibility of organizations and structure has given us a new vocabulary in which such words as "decline," "insecurity," and "disorganization" are prominent. Our faith in the stability of individuals is weakening. In fact, we are embracing an ideology of lament. We see families disintegrating before our eyes. Small communities are no longer the seat of residential living. Moral estrangement and spiritual isolation seem to pervade our culture. Even athletics has fallen prey to greed. Such a world will not conquer its loneliness through communities of faith which feed personal neuroses instead of presenting the ethical teachings of Jesus.

But the biblical witness does not offer this kind of a picture. Scripture doesn't speak of great "watered down" movements of palatable Christianity. Rather it speaks of

morally tough religious *minorities*. Paul speaks of Christians as a *colony*, a group of pioneers thrown out into an
unchristian world. Christians pioneer a new life-style.

Isaiah also spoke of religion as a minority group. He
used the word "remnant," a little group which in a time
that is surrendering old values under the pressure of a
passing generation preserves authentic spiritual values for
children yet unborn. Pioneer and remnant; remnant and
pioneer. The tension is always there: pioneering the better
and preserving the best; tough little groups of committed
Christians.

Fortunately our morally tough little communities of
faith do not have to start from scratch. We have a rich
legacy to draw from. The prophets and Jesus aimed at the
right target, the people within the religious community.
Whereas religion had prayed for outsiders, Jesus emphasized praying for ourselves, using the pronoun "our father," and praying, not like the publican who thanked God
he wasn't like "ordinary" people, but like the sinner who
saw his own need so clearly.

The testimony and life witness of the Christian community is the key to conquering loneliness. Dr. Samuel
Johnson observed that "testimony has great weight and
casts the balance." And the testimony of a life is the contribution Jesus made to religion. *Jesus, frankly, gave the
world few new meanings of religious thought.* Distinguished church historian Adolf Harnack gave a series of
lectures in the Great Hall of the University of Berlin on
the meaning of Christianity. He summed up the meaning
of Christianity in three articles: (1) the fatherhood of God;
(2) the infinite worth of every human soul; and (3) the
triumph of the Kingdom of God.[1]

We would have to admit that those articles are what Jesus taught. Over and over he stressed the fatherhood of God—his model prayer emphasized the father; his parable of the prodigal son stressed father and son as God-man encounter; and over and over he stressed the infinite worth of every human soul. His parables of the lost sheep and the lost coin and the experience with the thief on the cross and many others pointed to that article. Finally, over and over, Jesus stressed the triumph of the Kingdom of God.

None of these three essentials of faith began with Jesus, not a single one. In ancient Egypt, reforming Pharaoh Ikhnaton proclaimed one God, the father of men. The Hebrew prophets defended the same doctrine. As for the idea of worth of every human soul, the Stoic philosophers defended the same doctrine. And before Jesus ever began his ministry, the Roman poet Virgil in his Fourth Ecologue prophesied a kingdom of heaven.[2] None of the three elements of Christianity were original with Jesus.

The teaching of Jesus was presented with the persuasiveness of his personal example. He lived it. He was a doer. He didn't simply shout good advice; he pointed to a God who is a doer, a worker. He brought into our experience a God who does more than stand up in heaven and shout good advice. He initiated a presence of God among morally tough enclaves of Christians. His Beatitudes are actually messages of encouragement and forgiveness for all who take his absolute moral demands seriously. Love is itself described as a kind of moral activity.

Because of this there exists an ethical mandate in our attempt to conquer loneliness. Loneliness is resolved through communities of faith, but if the resolution is to be resolved in a Christian manner, it will be accomplished by people who care deeply about the concerns and conditions of people around them.

4.

LONELINESS
and the
Discovery of Satisfaction

Exposure to the Highest and Best

We are goal-striving creatures, continually setting goals because we stop struggling without them. Without the goal of literacy, few of us would make the effort to struggle out of bed early in the morning to get our children off to school. Without the goal of passing grades, most of us wouldn't go through the agony of prodding our children to do homework.

But what amazes me is that few of us bother to set goals for overcoming loneliness. In fact, one of the great tragedies of life is that we tend to settle for a lot less love and solitude in our lives than we could have if we possessed the strength and the will to work for more. Indeed, the Scriptures encourage us to exercise a little "management-by-objectives" even when it comes to our Christian perspective.

One of the most cordial and affectionate letters we have from the hand of the Apostle Paul was addressed to the

Christians at Philippi in Macedonia. This was the first congregation established through the Apostle on European soil. He was careful to explain to these people the tremendous difference it makes in our lives when we deliberately expose ourselves to the highest and best instead of the lowest and worst. Paul put it this way, "Finally, brethren, whatever is true, whatever is honorable, whatever is just, whatever is pure, whatever is lovely, whatever is gracious, if there is any excellence, if there is anything worthy of praise, think about these things" (Phil. 4:8).

In other words, Paul is urging the Philippians to cultivate their religious emotions through setting some positive spiritual goals for themselves. Religious awareness is essential to spiritual health. We cannot conquer loneliness and develop meaning in life by simply receiving a transfusion of ego-strength once or twice a year, like a person going to the hospital to get a blood transfusion when his or her body needs it. Rather, we must have a permanent day-by-day, week-by-week association with healthy people and healthy thoughts. We must develop some inner capacity for conquering our loneliness without having to depend on earth-shaking transfusions of emotionalism.

Positive Approaches to Loneliness Factors

Dr. William Glasser has written a marvelous book entitled *Positive Addiction*.[1] In it he makes the point that all addiction need not be negative. We tend to think of an addict as one who is "hooked" on alcohol, drugs, food, sex, or cigarettes. These negative addictions which many people enjoy in spite of the harm it does them are quite common. But Glasser maintains that it is possible to become addicted to things that do us good. Exercise, running, meditation, thinking, and a host of other good qualities in life are also addictive, and can become so much a part of life that in their absence we feel pain, misery, discomfort, anxiety, or guilt. Like all addictions, the suffering is relieved only by resumption of the addicting activity.

Positive addiction is a real possibility. My own approach to writing has become addictive. When I was in high school, I paid little attention to academic pursuits. In fact, I graduated in the bottom half of my class. Through the persistence of the football coach, I gained admission to Furman University, and there, thanks to some tutoring from roommates and much personal effort, I managed to make it. In fact, I managed to get a scholarship to the Divinity School at Harvard University. Up to that point, however, my vocabulary was quite limited. Consequently, I had to struggle hard with written assignments and term papers.

When my first semester at Harvard began, I realized that in order to remain a student in good standing I was going to have to write, and write prolifically. But how could I write when my vocabulary was quickly and easily exhausted on almost any subject?

That fall I happened to read a copy of the *Autobiography of Malcolm X*. I discovered that at one time he had been the victim of a very limited vocabulary. In his efforts to improve he purchased a dictionary, and night after night he copied words into a notebook. Beginning with "a" he worked himself through the entire dictionary.

I decided that might work for me too, so I copied words from the dictionary for one hour each evening into the pages of a notebook. The process produced boredom, impatience, and regret. Besides that, it was time-consuming. Sheer will power carried me through the first few months. Then, I began to get addicted to verbalization and writing, and in time I actually looked forward to term papers, and I selected courses which required them.

Even after graduating from the doctoral program at Vanderbilt University, I remained "hooked." I wrote and published article after article, sermon after sermon. But they didn't satisfy my addiction, so I turned to writing books. I am now to the point that I can't go a week without writing something, and when I stop, I experience pain, misery, discomfort, and anxiety.

In a similar way, the positive addiction process can create a better life for our spiritual emotions. Several years ago I spent two weeks in Miami, Florida, studying in a specialized program in addictive sciences, sponsored by the University of Miami School of Medicine. My Miami roommate, Stan, is a professor of pharmacology from Samford University in Birmingham, Alabama. A dedicated Lutheran layman, he has established a regular procedure for a few moments of meditation each day to combat loneliness through attempting to affirm the meaningfulness of his life for that particular day. Every morning for a few minutes he sits on the side of his bed and spends a few minutes reading a little devotional magazine published by his denomination. Stan told me that when he first started this, he had to force himself to do it. But now that early morning period of meditation is far more than a habit; it is a positive addiction.

It takes a considerable amount of self-discipline to become positively addicted to something. In order to be successful it must be something we want to do, a goal we want to meet—not something we are forced to do by others. If someone had chased me with a gun and tried to get me positively addicted to writing, it would not have been successful. If someone had forced Stan to have moments of meditation, I don't think that would have been successful either.

Glasser, in his research on positive addiction, notes that the most common benefit people receive from their addiction is a sense of confidence.[2] So, when we miss doing it, we lose an essential part of our being.

Within a church fellowship there are people who have become positively addicted to the life of the church. If something deprives them of the fellowship, "life doesn't seem quite right" and they are severely threatened emotionally and spiritually.

The Search for New Directions

A doctor friend once told me that after over twenty-five years of practice he didn't believe that vocational success provides lasting satisfaction and lasting self-acceptance. I believe this can be affirmed by millions of lonely people today. In addition, our frenetic scramble for money and status doesn't produce happiness.

But so often we fantasize an imagined paradise in which status and money wipe out all loneliness and feelings of alienation and set the stage for satisfying friendships and a life of pleasure. Sometimes our failing self-acceptance prods us to search for new settings, friends, and attainments with the idea that we will meet nicer and more powerful people who will really appreciate and understand us. Raymond Chapman, professor in the London School of Economics, has observed that the "symbol of success is no longer the mansion on a hill but the more spacious drawing-room for entertaining more gracious people. . . . Somewhere there must be people who are not insecure and lonely. . . . It is only money that keeps us from being one of them." [3] Unfortunately this kind of thinking is reflected and perpetuated through much commercial advertising. When we are bombarded by statements that what adds life is a Coke, that salvation comes with owning a Datsun, that the king who is coming is not a Christ figure but a beer, and that miracles for monks come from Xerox and not God, then we must admit that commercial advertising is tremendously potent in patterning our thinking. We have become victims of a distorted view of life which ignores authentic relationships and produces loneliness in the midst of a crowd.

It seems to me, however, that loneliness—lack of purposeful activity and meaningful relationships—demands far more attention than it has received. Academic and research attention has mainly been on the biological study of humans for life prolongation rather than for satisfaction and meaningfulness in life. It is to be hoped that we will soon grasp the importance of researching the quality of life with the same intensity and depth as researching cancer and disease. Perhaps we would then expose the bogus claims of status and materialism and affirm the revival of spiritual and personal values. But as one American girl concluded, "Spiritual goals in life are a lot harder to attain than a Cadillac." [4]

Lost Victories

Have you ever been involved in a situation in which you achieved a victory but your personal losses were so great as to make the victory seem like a defeat? I have. My first year in college, freshmen athletes were not permitted by the NCAA to play on varsity squads. Consequently we participated on freshman teams. That fall our Furman freshman football team journeyed to Banner Elk, North Carolina, to play Lees-McRae Junior College. Lees-McRae possessed a fine team; they were the number-one-ranked junior college in the nation at that time.

Now, Banner Elk is certainly no metropolitan area, and as we rode through that small mountain town, all we saw were the college and a huge, beautiful, modern hospital that serves the surrounding Appalachian communities. We happened to win the athletic contest by a single point. But it was a brutal game and we had to return to our university campus without six of our starters who remained behind in that hospital. On the bus trip back to our university campus, our mood was hardly that of victors. It seemed like a defeat, so great had been the cost. We gladly would have traded the victory for the health of our six players, if that had been possible.

Ancient culture called such situations Pyrrhic victories. The victory is really a loss. Many of our great triumphs of materialism and religion in the last decade have been Pyrrhic victories.

I have known people who would willingly relinquish all the money earned in their lifetime if they could reclaim the failure of a son or daughter who was neglected by them as a child. Many an adult would willingly give up a coveted vocational position for a lesser one if they could reclaim the potential and time in a once-loving relationship that ended in divorce. Sometimes the price of obtaining the imagined paradise is far too high. Indeed, many of us who try to find what this world calls "life" actually wind up losing the very life we have. Such situations are reflected in a kind of loneliness that is driving many people to seek easy solutions to complex problems. Pyrrhic victories are horrible realities and create superficial religious involvement.

Do you remember several years ago when thalidomide hit the market in Europe? It was designed to eliminate the symptoms of morning sickness in pregnant women, but it did something else as well. Hundreds of mothers took the drug and discovered too late that they had given birth to infants whose arms and legs had not developed. What a horrible situation. The cure for the stressful symptoms of morning sickness turned out to be worse than the discomfort.

This often happens in religious life as a product of stressful situations. Many of our religious escape techniques can turn out to be worse than the loneliness from which we try to escape.

Loneliness, Christianity, and Satisfaction

As perhaps never before, our society seems to be obsessed with the need to feel and act secure. The strain of this pretense is breaking down the mental balance of many people. We often become divided selves: on one hand we profess Christian beliefs in greater numbers and frequence; on the other hand we are faced with the overarching questions raised by science and our world's stockpile of nuclear weapons. Satisfaction appears to be such an impossible task until we abdicate our efforts to become whole people. We divide our hours into the social, personal, vocational, and religious, never allowing our religious feelings to penetrate our friendships, jobs, and families. We then expect our religious leaders to address only a portion of our existence.

Admiral Rickover has viewed our loneliness in these terms: "We find ourselves a people whose bellies are full, but whose spirits are empty." My friend Charles Kao has noted that the twentieth-century person has been characterized by a cartoonist as a tall, well-dressed, well-fed, well-developed person looking out over a wide landscape at a huge question mark which hangs over the distant horizon.[5] This person has an incalculable future. Without meaningful relationships and purposeful activity that future becomes a puzzle. Adding to that confusion is a world full of voices without meaning and purpose. Consequently the bewildered person is driven to excesses in alcohol, drugs, and religion which promise relief from the unbearable ambiguity and loneliness.

There must be a place where this twentieth-century person's pilgrimage can find meaning and purpose to enable the vision of the future to be a clear one. The roots of past security and the perspective of the future must merge to inform the pilgrimage. Consequently an understanding of satisfaction is essential for conquering loneliness.

But how do we achieve this undergirding satisfaction? Is it possible? Surely; others appear to have attained it. Certainly the Christian faith of the apostle Paul pulled his life together, integrated it, made it sound, and saved him from a split and aimless life. Jesus of Nazareth also appeared to be fulfilled, to have within him something stable which gave him calmness in the face of the loneliness and uncertainty of his day. *How do we* attain the *same satisfaction?*

According to Jesus, the deepest hell a person can fall into would be to have everything to live *with* and nothing to live *for.* Jesus' teachings focus on the *ends* of life. I believe they have little direct contribution to make to the means by which we live. Jesus' means were vastly different from ours. The Bible says nothing about euthanasia, modern medicine, and jet travel. The contributions of Scripture concern the *ends* of life, what people live *for.* As we have discussed, it still holds true that if we gain a wealth of means and lose our ends, it profits us little and leaves us lonelier than ever.

When we compare ourselves with previous generations in terms of our *means* of living, we certainly seem to have reached the ultimate. But when we turn our gaze to the *ends* for which we live, we see a different picture. Harry Emerson Fosdick is right, "We have improved our means to an unimproved end." [6]

In our pilgrimage we have trusted inventive science. It is indeed magnificent, but now we have come to see that instead of solving human problems, the power furnished by science complicates them. Again and again the question rises: what moral quality will control that power and to what end? The science which can heat our homes, cook our food, and power our motor vehicles can also be used to arm weapons and destroy human life.

Consider also the power of education. Education can mold minds or destroy them. Perhaps the most educated nation in the past century was Nazi Germany. The question still arises: great means and power, but what about the ends?

Consider history, that whole panorama of human experience. And then turn attention to that little group of disciples and their master teacher in Galilee. Their *means* of living was "crude." The swiftest travel they possessed was a donkey. Their houses, roughed out of stone or brick, had one room and possibly a small window. The family slept on a high platform and the animals slept on the floor. By our standards of housing, those little holes of existence would be called poverty-stricken. But think of the *ends* for which those people lived! The impact of their lives revolutionized the world.

Then there were the ancient Greeks, a people small in numbers but great in mind. They were crudely primitive in their means. But consider their *ends*. Their world was influenced by Egyptians who spent fortunes preserving dead bodies, by Assyrians who worshiped gods that were half animal, by hoards of people so illiterate they had to carry weapons everywhere they went. Against that kind of world, the Greeks behaved civilly and thoughtfully. They drew no racial, social, or national barriers, and fostered thinkers like Plato and Sophocles who lived for great ends.[7]

Into that Greek culture walked a man named Paul the Apostle who had abandoned the rituals of Judaism and Jewish exclusiveness. Paul looked around and liked what he saw. These people had never met Jesus so their *means* to religion missed the mark but their *ends* were on target. Paul told those sophisticated thinkers of Athens that he could see they were a religious people—their ends were in tune with those of Christianity. Then he proceeded to tell them specifically about the "unknown God" whose existence they recognized but did not understand. And while Paul was there he learned from their culture and then set out to extend his preaching of the gospel of Christ. The Greeks were crudely primitive in many ways, but when we think of their ends, the things for which they lived, they move up into a position in the spiritual history of humanity that Los Angeles, New York, Chicago, and Washington may never achieve.

But progress is not a continuous movement throughout history. It is not automatic and certainly is not expressed chiefly in mechanical inventions. Beethoven is not to be considered less great in comparison to a modern musician because he did not own a hearing aid. Nor are some of our theological mentors of the past less great in comparison to us because they did not have church gymnasiums, electronic amplifying equipment, and the ability to cross the country in three hours. The means of life are not the domain of Christianity.

When Reinhold Niebuhr prayed the now famous "Serenity Prayer," he was preaching in a little church in Massachusetts. Just a handful of people were in the audience. Someone liked the prayer and after the service asked him for a copy. It was written on a crumpled-up piece of paper. Niebuhr said, "Here, I doubt I'll have any more use for it." The prayer became the most published prayer in America and Alcoholics Anonymous adopted it as their theme.

I recall the stories of Harry Emerson Fosdick and Walter Rauschenbush working under extremely difficult conditions in the slums of New York City—and of the crude implements of Schweitzer in primitive Africa. Such pitiful means, but think of the ends for which they lived!

The Beatitudes, as recorded in Matthew's Gospel, do not speak of a life-style that guarantees a comfortable and improved style of life. They may reap such as a by-product but there's no assurance of it. Meekness, service, righteousness, mercy, peacemaking, and purity of heart are difficult ends to live for. But Jesus is correct: they do bring the ultimate in happiness and satisfaction.

How, then, do we conquer loneliness and attain purposeful activity and meaningful relationships? I believe this comes through improving the ends for which we live, through recognizing the gift of life from God which enables us to open our hearts to people regardless of their social stature. In this way, we are enabled to transform the question mark of the future into an exclamation point as we march along life's pilgrimage with purpose and meaning. We become *other*-directed instead of self-directed.

The philosopher Immanuel Kant gave us this story of Carazan, a pious miser. It seems one evening as he was going over his accounts, calculating profits, he fell asleep and saw the Angel of Death coming for him. At that moment he realized that his destiny was cast and that to all the good he had done nothing could be added, and from all the evil he had committed, nothing could be taken away. The Angel of Death carried Carazan to the heavens, and there a voice spoke to him, "Carazan, your service of God is rejected. You have closed your heart to the love of man, and have clutched your treasures with an iron grip. You have lived only for yourself, and therefore you shall also live the future in eternity alone and removed from all communion with the whole of creation." At that instant he was driven through the universe toward eternal silence, loneliness, and darkness. He finally lost all sight of light. He would always be looking ahead into the infinite abyss of darkness, without help or hope of any return. In the agony of that moment, he threw out his hands with such force that he awoke. That dream shook Carazan into reality. In response he said, ". . . now I have been taught to esteem mankind; for in that terrifying solitude I would have preferred even the least of those whom in the pride of my fortune I had turned from my door to all the treasures of (the world) ." [8]

On Not Getting Lost in the Crowd

Shortly after arriving in Waco, Texas, as minister to a large Baptist congregation, I began the difficult and time-consuming task of reading the mail that had accumulated in the pastor's office. One letter came from a denominational office and it was obviously a form letter. An IBM machine had typed in my name and address to try to make it appear to be an original, personal letter. The body of the letter began like this: "Since you are the pastor of one of our convention's largest churches, we know that you will be interested in the following." The letter continued, "We are sending this message to the prestigious pastors in our state." As I read the rest of the material, it became apparent to me that value judgments had been made regarding the theological thrust, power, interest, and persuasion of our church based solely upon its size. This is the price we pay for our society's worship of size. But quantity or size is an utterly fallacious standard when trying to estimate power.

Whether we consciously express it or not, this matter of how small is large/how large is small, cuts at the very fabric of our Christian pilgrimage and the accompanying issue of loneliness. Recently I discovered a delightful little book entitled *Mister God, This is Anna* by Fynn.[9] Five-year-old Anna has a charming and incisive mind, and she is wrestling with the idea that Mister God does not at all mind making himself small: "People who think that Mister God is very, very big make a big mistake. Mister God can be any size he wants to be. Mister God is one who has not just one point of view but an infinity of viewing points. Consequently if the whole purpose of our living is to be like Mister God, we too must make ourselves small sometimes."

To be sure, Mister God *can* be any size. So can the communities which embrace God. Some years ago, J. B. Phillips wrote a book entitled *Your God Is Too Small*. This insightful idea made quite an impact on Christian thinking, but after viewing much of contemporary culture and modern society, I'm of the opinion that someone should write a book entitled "Your God Is Too Big!" Certainly, today, we Americans cannot be accused of worshiping smallness. Rather, we seem to equate power and worth to big buildings, big crowds, and big corporations.

But this phenomenon has surfaced frequently in religious history. Because of their experiences in slavery and lack of security, the Hebrew people at one point feared being hemmed in. They developed a theology of bigness. The Psalmist repeatedly sings of the Lord's deliverance as being led into large places. The 18th Psalm states: "He brought me forth also into a large place. He delivered me because he delighted in me" (v. 19). The 118th Psalm reads: "I called upon the Lord in distress. The Lord answered me and set me in a large place" (v. 5). Security, for the Psalmist, was equated with largeness.

During the days of the Hebrew prophets, this attitude was questioned. In fact, a central thrust of the prophetic word was the assertion that size was not an indication either of truth or immortality. Merely enlarging the setting did not lift one out of the littleness of his or her thinking. Bigger worship was not necessarily better worship. Much of the rage of the prophetic message was directed at Israel's concept of the *bigness* of religion. Image had replaced integrity and the voice of God spoke out to put things back in their proper perspective.

Religious perception often confuses the righteousness of its cause with the worship of size. One of the great scorekeepers in religious history was the prophet Elijah. He was always looking over his shoulder at the size of other religious cults, the numbers in their worship services, and the apparent potency of their effort. Consequently, Elijah's life was a constant roller-coaster ride—euphoria when his crowd appeared to be the largest and total loneliness when it seemed to him that Baal had more prophets than God. In fact, Elijah spent a rather large portion of his life reacting to the activities in other religious communities instead of concentrating on the assets God had provided him with. This spiritual paranoia generated frequent waves of self-pity in Elijah's life. Then as now, any person who goes around pitying himself bores others with the stories of his troubles. So people began to leave Elijah more and more to himself, and his loneliness engulfed him. Eventually there was no one around to listen to his troubles and we find a bitterly discouraged Elijah falling asleep under a broom tree.

Then God sent a message to that despondent scorekeeper, "Get up and eat." So Elijah put aside his worry about the size of other cults and began his personal quest for God. And in that quest Elijah found that the power of God could not be discerned through counting numbers of believers. The world's standard of measurement is not that of God's. Consequently, a great and strong wind rent the mountains with force and power, but no God was discernible. An earthquake shook the ground on which Elijah stood. Again, God could not be discerned. Then, a fire appeared with great brilliance, but again no God was there. And after the fire came the still, small voice of God.

I'm certain that after that day Elijah's definition of the size of God was greatly altered, and his conceptualization of his own resources and worth was heightened.

In reading the Gospels we find that the disciples were impressed by the crowds which followed Jesus. But there is no hint that Jesus was impressed by the size of his audience. In fact, most of the parables of Jesus rebuked our cult of bigness and noise. He talked about the little bit of leaven which a woman hid in three measures of meal, of faith the size of a mustard seed. He encouraged his disciples to be the salt of the earth, to give zest to life. He taught that whoever wanted to be the largest in that scramble for divine affirmation must be servant of all.

I am fascinated by the realization that Jesus didn't feel lonely because his group was small. His life and ministry didn't need sensationalism or bigness, but his appeal was for his followers to be like mustard seed, salt, and leaven. In fact, just a small amount of any of these is effective out of all proportion to its size. The original meaning of the word *church—ecclesia—*is "called out," a minority selected from the majority to be the leaven of influence on surrounding society.

The power to conquer loneliness is in that kind of "called-out" body, an inner group of men and women who have been genuinely kindled by Christ's spirit and are living and thinking above the average and ahead of the time. Christian community can embrace the God who is small enough to relate to us in an intimate and creative way.

Scripture records that religious meaning is like a precious pearl that is hidden. Sometimes we stumble upon it quite by accident. We wander upon it like a poor man in a field, fall upon it, and in joy grab it and take it. In other cases, the precious pearl is found only after great expenditures of time and energy, like a merchant spending his time and money in a long expedition. Finding the meaning of life in that case is no accident.

However we find it, stumbling upon it or searching for it, it is of incalculable value to find a Christian community which meets our needs and conquers our loneliness in an intelligent and accurate way. Some of us stumbled into our positive Christian communities, others went through the agonies of time and disillusionment to uncover the perspective that is ours. If we have not affirmed the value in our Christian growth experience, touched base with the potential that is within us, and are engaged in searching for meaning in the might and power of the world's structures and viewpoints, perhaps our God wishes for us to reach out and discover the satisfaction that is available to us through purposeful activity and meaningful relationships.

5.

LONELINESS
and the
Discovery of Love
and Healing

Clarification of Love Language

Merely coming together under the umbrella of pious rhetoric is not the answer to lingering loneliness. In fact, many marriage and family counselors believe that the most intense loneliness is frequently found in families where communication has broken down. Consequently, to speak of love, healing, and intimacy without probing beyond the language and the structures means very little.

"Love-language" is common in our church experience. Yet love-language is not found as often in the New Testament as we might expect. There are no occurrences *at all* of the noun *love* in Mark, Acts, Titus, James, or 1 and 2 Peter. In fact, the use of the word *love* in the New Testament is only ten percent attributable to Jesus. Love is a magnificent and powerful concept, but little is really said about it in Scripture. For this reason, as we continue our effort to combat the powerful force of loneliness with the more powerful force of love, we must examine the theological base for our search.

The Assertiveness of Intimate Love

Myron Madden has written a book entitled *The Power to Bless* in which he says that Christians have been characterized as the "people of the blessing." And I believe we are supposed to live among people who bless us, affirm us, and create a climate of authentic intimacy. Divine love has an intimate and universal character as Jesus knew it. He pictured his father as an intimate God, one who cares about the grass, one who is aware of the welfare of a common sparrow, and one who knows the number of hairs on our heads.

Church, as positive Christian community combatting loneliness, then, is concerned with living out and reflecting that kind of intimate love. Scripture tells us that love is the very bond of unity that makes people a church. *How, then, do we create a place where people can be loved without being devoured and can attain freedom without being abandoned?*

As I think of "love," I am amazed at how Jesus loved people in an assertive, unconditioned manner as opposed to the passive love of the Pharisees. Israel Abrahams, a Jewish scholar, has written a book (*Studies in Pharisaism and the Gospels*) comparing the witness to God of the Pharisees with that of the early Christians. He has noted that in Pharisaism there was real hesitation, if not refusal, to make the return of the sinner too easy. The initiative in seeking the love of God was supposed to be left to the sinner, not to God. On the other hand, Jesus' love for individuals was more inclined toward taking the initiative, toward reaching out to touch those who had not been touched. Consequently, there is a different kind of love expressed in the actions of Jesus. It's not the kind of love that

says, "Here I am as God's representative; come to me."
Rather, *it is an assertive, outward, reaching, initiating
brand of blessing.* Consequently, the church it created was
not one destined merely to exist as a symbol and sanctuary
for those strongly motivated to seek its shelter. On the contrary, it was vested on the premise that lack of love is lack
of authentic being.

Small wonder, then, that Jesus referred to the Pharisees
in his day as creators of heavy yokes for people to wear. In
Jesus' time, carpenters made both yokes and plows. Un-
doubtedly Jesus and Joseph had experience in making
them. Such yokes were not confined to cattle; they were
used on human beings who had been taken captive in war.
Slaves were also kept under a real yoke of iron or wood.
These practices had a long history among the Jewish people and the yoke had long been spoken of as a symbol of
subjection and servitude. Consequently, when Jesus called
his yoke of obedience easy as compared to the Pharisees'
brand of obedience, the meaning is clear: a love that will
not reach out to a sinner places a yoke of servitude around
the sinner's neck. The lack of a blessing is a form of en-
slavement.

Perhaps the first thing, then, that needs to be done to fulfill our desire to be a community of love is to bring our love
to the situations in which people live. No one individual
possesses enough resources to cope with all of life by himself or herself.

If there is a need in our world today, it is for human
beings to work to reach out to one another in assertive love.
The great preacher Henry Ward Beecher put it this way:
"Religion means work; religion means work in a dirty
world; religion means peril; blows given, blows taken as
well. . . ." Love is reaching out to those who sit emotion-

ally starved. Mere statements about love and symbols of love will never take the place of reaching out in face-to-face relationships with our neighbors.

I supervised a senior project for a black Harvard student who pastors a church in New York City. The project proposal was a rather ambitious plan to devise an outreach program to the city through mass mailings, a radio broadcast ministry, and a cassette tape subscription plan. Armed with a sound education which concentrated on media and preaching, my student advisee was set to tackle the outreach plan with the fervor of a public relations manager. Somewhat to his dismay, and I must confess to my partial delight, his church's governing board vetoed the rather impersonal plan in favor of concentrating on the shut-in members in a nursing home who had never been approached by the minister and church with outreaching, face-to-face Christian love.

Our neighbors deserve our personal attention, our expressions of presence, not our detached opinions and ideas. They deserve our initiative. The story is told of a little child who was awakened one night in the middle of a thunderstorm. As the lightning flashed and the thunder clapped, the frightened child called his parents. Both mother and father ran in, calmed the child, and assured him that "God is here, it's okay." After several minutes the thunder struck again. The child screamed, "Mother, Father, come here. I know God is here, but I want somebody with skin on them." Indeed, a concept is not enough to hold to in tough times!

We did not enter this world on our own. Mutuality was the process from the very beginning. Two other people conceived and gave birth to us. Many more cared for us during our times of vulnerability. Without these numerous outside resources, none of us would have survived. And the way we began characterizes the way in which the Creator expects us to live. Without those who reach out to love us, we are unfulfilled and lonely. Love is not a disembodied ideal; it is the mutual involvement of persons. One cannot become a whole person without becoming involved in that kind of love. Christian love is relational. Therefore, it is not passive.

Love without Limits

A second hallmark of Christian love is *tolerance.* In Jesus' time, members of the Jewish synagogue lived according to the law. The law had an answer for every problem of life, but it depersonalized people and its interpretation was narrow-gauged. If a person had a problem he or she was presented with a patent answer. The individual need was subordinated to the needs of the institution.

Love which depersonalizes people is not Christian love, although it is true that in many ways the Christian community has depersonalized people. We have too often presented people as targets for the institution. At times the church resembles a company that wants to sell its merchandise in whatever way possible and whose main concern is to find a weakness through which the merchandise can be thrust on the customer. For example, I have known ministers who act like the vacuum cleaner salesmen who must prove to a housewife that her domestic happiness depends on the cleaner's being demonstrated for her. Sometimes we spend more time convincing people they have needs to be met with what we can comfortably hand out than with responding to their actual needs and concerns.

As with a salesman, the effectiveness of a minister is sometimes measured in numbers—number of dollars in the budget, number of new members, number of baptisms. I remember a story the popular character Charlie Weaver (in real life Cliff Arquette) told about a brother who could read numbers, but could not read letters. Someone asked Weaver if this presented problems. "Well," he answered, "when he's traveling and sees road signs, he can tell you how far it is but he doesn't know *where* to!" Sometimes this strange ability some ministers and congregations possess to read numbers but not destinations tends to treat people as if they were targets for a product the church is trying to push on them. The love is not unconditional, without limits, but conditioned on the basis of a response. Several years ago a church in Indiana actually released "One Thousand Resurrection Helium Balloons" at Easter. The balloons contained gift certificates ranging in value from $.50 to $50. In order to be validated, the certificates had to be presented at Sunday school on Easter Sunday! [1]

Such gimmicks are not the methodology of Christian faith. The Scriptures so frequently go against such concepts and practices. They tell us that a group of people gathered at a place called Babel to try to erect a monument to themselves. Every working moment was spent trying to build a tower greater than anyone had ever built. All their efforts and money were pumped into that project. "Come," they exclaimed, "let us build ourselves a tower with its top in the heavens, and let us make a name for ourselves." Such splendor, of course, did not eventuate. In fact, the entire enterprise was most displeasing to God, as all limited perceptions of greatness are.

A most appealing thing about many churches is the apparent warmth and closeness of community found within them. The members seem to care deeply about each other. But, unfortunately, their caring has boundaries. People outside the charmed circle of the born-again believers are viewed only as rivals or as targets for conversion. In such instances, the desired result is not to express love and care and concern, but to charm the outsider into the exclusive inner circle.

Tolerance of those outside the caring circle is hard to find in today's world. And tragically, today's television has contributed immeasurably to our distorted concept of community. James A. Taylor, a Canadian editor, has given us unique insights into television's concept of a caring circle or community.[2] Story after story projects a love that has limits. The caring group affirms itself while attacking others. Starsky and Hutch genuinely care about each other. They shed tears over their misfortunes and the predicaments of their friends. The same is true of Charlie's Angels, and other televized caricatures of fighters for law and order. But outside their own circle, caring stops; for opponents there is only hostility. These are two models—yesterday's Pharisees and today's television "whodunnits"—which seem to explain how Christians and churches can proclaim love but produce hate; create warm fellowship but also generate frustration.

Taylor is right about television: (1) the characters do not develop and (2) any change is not growth but instant conversion. Archie Bunker is just as bigoted today as five years ago. Rhoda, Laverne and Shirley, and Frank Burns do not seem to have matured at all as a result of their marital and personal problems. And when characters do change, it's not through development. They simply change sides. They get converted. A safe-cracker with high principles switches sides and helps the police. A reluctant drug-pusher changes sides and becomes an instant hero. An entrapped prostitute joins the "good guys." All that is needed is the right kind of persuasion. They find in the "good guys" what they could not find in crime, prostitution, and drugs. They are the same people, with the same aims. But now they have switched sides. That's been the appeal to the audience in both television and church. Instant love. Change sides.

Such conversion episodes are laudable, but unrealistic. Most people do not respond to life in instant upheavals. Certainly, in our mass media world which promotes those who "change sides" and become instant religious heroes, it is the most merchandisable form of Christianity. The media serves instant love instead of percolating it. But Jesus maintained that Christians are recognized by their loving actions, not their street-corner boasts. Society's real religious heroes and heroines are those people who have coped with life and grown wiser and more perceptive. Jesus sought changed lives but rendered an accurate presentation of the tolerant, assertive, and *developmental* nature of Christian love, even to the point of telling many to "go home" and work their love there. Even our saints are possessed with clay feet. We should not visualize utopian Christian settings which will only break and leave us searching either for another saint to follow temporarily or for another methodology for conquering loneliness. Thus it remains for us to consider the dynamic nature of divine reality and the attendant dynamic nature of a loving Christian community.

The Dynamic Nature of Loving Community

Scripture emphasizes character development. Strong characters face crises, cope with them, and in their efforts grow and develop. They grow wiser, sadder, richer, poorer, more perceptive, and even more bitter. But they grow and they change. Abraham, Moses, David, Solomon, Jeremiah, Matthew, Peter, Paul—their characters develop as they grow and they learn.

For example, consider the vivid portrayal in Scripture

of the growth of King David. God's personal choice to command the chosen people, he unified Israel and Judah, and removed Canaanite power from the land. But that leader's personal life was in constant development. The David and Bathsheba affair is graphically presented in the Bible. Having seen the beautiful Bathsheba while she was bathing, David sent for her and had sexual relations with her. Shortly thereafter, Bathsheba notified David she was pregnant. In an effort to cover his tracks, he eliminated Bathsheba's husband, Uriah, in a dastardly plan. Finally, David is confronted by Nathan, the prophet, and confesses his sin against God and humankind. Yet, such reconversion is hardly the end of the story. The child born by Bathsheba becomes sick and dies, plunging David into a depression of such depths that even the elders of his house cannot pull him from it. Again, David rises and goes into the house of God for worship. With renewed vigor he pursues leadership under God for his people. Then, he must witness the rebellion of a son in young adulthood who is killed in battle against David, prompting him to confess before God that he wished he had died instead of his son. Once again David rises and through the help of God becomes the leader of his people. There is a process of development and inspiration, not a one-time metamorphosis. Even the saints before us have walked where we must walk, through the valleys as well as on the mountaintops.

Conversely, a legal form of love and ostentation characterized the Pharisees in Jesus' day. They were the great preachers and teachers . . . they were "cool" and never "blew it." These Pharisees were expert at parading their piety by the use of in-language, by sounding a trumpet to attract a crowd to listen to their public prayers on street corners. And for all of this phoniness Jesus had nothing but the harshest of condemnation. He knew there was no authentic love and caring in their religious machinations—

this was the instant variety which can be turned on and off as it is convenient.

Notice, sharp in contrast, the developmental nature of love in the teachings of Jesus and Paul. The pivotal statement on love in the New Testament, 1 Corinthians 13, never does define love. Paul simply tells us how it works, how it develops. In this chapter Paul deals with certain defects of spirit and fellowship in the church. And *he uses himself as illustrative material for failure*. His glorification of love is actually an affirmation of God's presence in the pilgrimage of his life, through his valleys and his mountaintops.

My colleague and friend Paul Hanson understands divine activity as occurring through a model of "dynamic transcendence" which is a communal process. He contends that historical events do not constitute acts of God until they are interpreted by a Christian community. Events are seen as acts of God *only within a community of faith* as it relates the event to a confessional heritage which "supplies the context within which an unusual historical pattern of events can be perceived as part of a salvific plan moving in a purposeful direction." [3] This insight has proven helpful for me in understanding that the revelation of God is perceived through *the living faith of a community*. Christian love and healing are revealed only through the living faith of the Christian community. Thus the community of faith is our historical vessel for transmitting to a lonely modern world the healing power of God.

Healing Divisiveness

In George Bernard Shaw's play about Joan of Arc this haunting question is asked: "Is it necessary for every generation to burn its own Joan of Arc?" Divisiveness—bitter contention—has a long and sullied history in religious life.

What a cruel paradox this is: that which is meant for healing and wholeness becomes a source of acrid and shattering divisiveness, and in the process a climate of paralyzing loneliness clouds the atmosphere like a dense fog.

One of the earliest object lessons we have of this frightful condition is found in the biblical account of the relationship between the Samaritans and the Jews.

The Jewish religion had three major splits. The first split involved the Jews who lived in Egypt. They became so strong and self-confident that they defied the religious authorities at Jerusalem. They built their own temple on an island and held ceremonies similar to those in the temple in Jerusalem. (It was to this Jewish community that Mary and Joseph took the baby Jesus to escape the cruelty of Herod.)

Another temple became a strong rival of the Jewish temple at Jerusalem. This temple was built by the Samaritans at Schechem.

A tense rivalry had also developed between the Samaritan Jews and the Jerusalem Jews, and the Samaritans built their own temple on Mount Gerizim. They believed in Yahweh, acknowledged Moses as the founder of the faith, and accepted the Torah as the only authentic law. But they recognized Mount Gerizim as the chosen place of God instead of Jerusalem.

There is a historical basis for this difference of opinion. And as is so often the case in bitter controversy, there was an element of both right and wrong on both sides. Seldom is an issue clear-cut. But one of the monstrous tragedies of history is that so often non-Christian and Christian alike have been willing to massacre bodies and personalities over questionable issues. And the accumulated hate of the centuries between the Jews and the Samaritans vented its poison whenever contact between the two was made.

But Jesus set the prime example for all time in his role

as a peacemaker. The moving story of Jesus meeting and talking with the Samaritan woman at Jacob's well is a powerful indictment against racial and religious bigotry. After they talk, the woman points to Gerizim and says, "Sir, our fathers worshipped on this mountain, and you say Jerusalem is the place where people ought to worship." Jesus looks at her and replies, "Woman, the hour is coming when neither on this mountain nor in Jerusalem will you worship the Father." In other words, there is to be a new history, a new age, in which the wounds will be healed and the splits closed. The woman passes this amazing word to the villagers, and so many Samaritans show an interest that Jesus stays there with them for two days (John 4).

Luke tells the story of a similar crucial incident in Jesus' life. Approaching a Samaritan village, Jesus sent messengers ahead to let the people know he was coming. But the people refused to receive him because of his connection with Jerusalem. The rivalry was that strong! When the disciples realized this, they wanted God to send down fire from heaven and destroy the village. Imagine! They were ready to see people slaughtered for discourtesy and difference of opinion. Jesus rebuked them, insisting that he had not come to bring hurt but to save lives and heal wounds.

Over and over again Jesus hammers that message of healing love home to a divided world through his caring attention to people, his healings, and such stories as the one about the Good Samaritan. But let's put at least one of those healings into a larger context. You recall the marvelous and touching story of Jesus healing the ten lepers. Here were ten outcasts on the dump heap of society—shunned by everyone and lonely beyond anything we can imagine. But to Jesus they were injured, hurt, and sick human beings. Here is a poignant story of human misery in Luke 17. Jesus was moved, and with a word all ten were healed. But only one came to Jesus, thanked him and praised God—he was a Samaritan. Such irony. I believe Jesus' words reflect this: "Were not ten cleansed? Where are the nine? Was no one found to return and give praise to God except this foreigner?" Again and again we see Jesus exposing the Jewish and Samaritan split, exposing it for all that prejudice really is—ignorance and insensitivity.

The intensity of this Jewish feeling seems to peak in the story found in John 8. Jesus was talking to a group of Jews, and they weren't buying a word he said. In response Jesus accused them of not being God's children. This so infuriated them that they accused him of being a Samaritan who had a demon. What a charge—Jesus, a Samaritan! What hatred prejudice generates. And in this case the confrontation ended when the Jews tried to kill him with stones.

Even at the time of Jesus' return to heaven we find him once again trying to impress his listeners that divisiveness and its accompanying loneliness does not fit into his pattern of life. In Acts we read that forty days after the resurrection the disciples came together with Christ and asked him, "Lord, will you at this time restore the kingdom to *Israel?*" (Acts 1: 6) Jesus told them no. And he went on to say, ". . . You shall receive power when the Holy Spirit has come upon you; and you shall be my witnesses in Jersualem and all Judea and *Samaria* and to the end of the earth" (Acts 1: 8).

The life of Christ appears to have had a singular purpose: calling the people of his day back to a healthy, assertive form of religion. An intensive examination of Jesus' life can and will help us see that it is his intention for us to live together in peace within the Christian community.

There exist today in personalities massive holes of loneliness that could be plugged with the kind of healing com-

munity that a church should be. There are prejudices to
be overcome in our effort to attain solidarity with our
fellow human beings. We need to be reminded afresh of the
real meaning of Samaria. It can help us clarify our love
language, reaffirm the assertive nature of tolerant and intimate Christian love, and develop communities of faith
which can supply the confessional heritage to perceive the
acts of God in our day. Such understandings and perceptions are necessary for us to interpret where God is acting
in our day and to combat the loneliness which comes to us
all at various points in our existence.

Often as I ride along on an interstate highway I am
aware of the loads we must all bear, most especially when I
encounter a truck that takes up more than its share of the
highway. The truck bears a "wide load" sign, warning me
that I have to make more room for it to pass in safety.

In life, many people are forced to carry wide loads for a
portion of their journey. They have to carry more and pull
a little more responsibility than the rest of us. A caring,
healing community can give these people a little more
room to pass than does the often crass, proficient secular
world. The highway of God is very wide. At times all of
us must bear an illness or physical suffering and still try to
do our part for our family and our business.

In such times we need a community that will love us into
health by showing us a tolerance far beyond that of the
average group of people. As we march through a world of
death, separation, marital problems, rebellious children
and financial problems, as well as those rare but significant
moments of triumph, we can experience a peace and a cer-
tainty that we are not alone. A community of love and
healing undergirds our pilgrimage.

6.

LONELINESS
and the
Discovery of Prayer

A Very Present Reality

The blinding vision of loneliness has caused some of the greatest minds in history to retreat from the everyday secular world in an attempt to find the ultimate meaning of life. In the face of such retreat every activity seems futile. Leo Tolstoy expressed this reaction through one of his characters in *War and Peace:*

> Sometimes he remembered how he had heard that soldiers in war when entrenched under the enemy's fire, if they have nothing to do, try hard to find some occupation the more easily to bear the danger. . . . All men seemed like those soldiers, seeking refuge from life: some in ambition, some in cards, some in framing laws, some in women, some in toys, some in horses, some in politics, some in sport, some in wine and some in governmental affairs. "Nothing is trivial and nothing is important, it's all the same—only to save oneself from it as best one can . . . only not to see it, that dreadful it."

The tragic loneliness of human existence—the dreadful it—has caused people to search forever for someone or something to worship. Many have experienced this need in the fact that group activities do not touch the real question of loneliness. Without a relationship to Someone beyond human existence, our sense of belonging which groups give us disappears as soon as the group dissolves or we are separated from it. Even within the security of a group experience, we find ourselves contemplating ultimate reality.

In a recent class session we were discussing "death, dying, and loneliness." Two students representing theological traditions poles apart—Baptist and Unitarian—voiced similar perspectives. The Unitarian student from Michigan said, "Death is in your consciousness more than you feel comfortable with. Everything you're going through seems so inconsequential to your death." The black Baptist student from Mississippi pictured death as a "numb, dark experience with a continuous ringing noise." He confessed, "I think about being dead a great deal."

Regardless of our theological position we bring our fear of death into the temple, church, synagogue, fellowship, association, society, or house where we worship. Each of us tries to develop our own particular immortality formula.

In his Pulitzer prize-winning work, *The Denial of Death*, Ernest Becker describes the terror of ultimate loneliness in these words:

> What most people usually do is to follow one person's ideas and then another's, depending on who looms largest on one's horizon at the time. The one with the deepest voice, the strongest appearance, the most authority and success, is usually the one who gets our momentary allegiance; and we try to pattern our ideals after him. But as life goes on we get a perspective on this, and all these different versions of truth become a little pathetic. Each

person thinks that he has the formula for triumphing over life's limitations and knows with authority what it means to be a man, and he usually tries to win a following for his particular patent. Today we know that people try so hard to win converts for their point of view because it is more than merely an outlook on life: it is an immortality formula.[1]

The amazing force in life which we call "prayer" enables us to stand in the face of the threat of ultimate loneliness. Yet perhaps no force is more misunderstood or untapped than the spiritual force of prayer. Without prayer in its most effective form, the power to conquer loneliness is greatly diminished, if not actually defeated. Let's examine this significant personal and social power in our quest to conquer loneliness.

An insightful critic objected to Voltaire's writings on the ground that nothing could be so clear as Voltaire made it. An assessment on prayer runs the danger of the same criticism. Certainly prayer is not as clear as we attempt to make it. I meet and talk with many people who are having genuine problems coming to terms with the concept of prayer as communication with God. Some are groping in the dark, having lost trust in it. Others have come to think it is unnecessary. Still others are finding the seemingly conflicting claims of Scripture to be most confusing.

Biblical Complexities

Jesus Christ was a person of prayer. He prayed at every serious crisis in his public career. Even the last words on the cross were words of prayer in which he committed his spirit. Jesus left some staggering affirmations about prayer: "I tell you, whatever you ask in prayer, believe that you will receive it and you will" (John 14: 14); "Whatever you ask in prayer, you will receive, if you have faith" (Matt. 21: 22) .

These are magnificent promises. Yet, usually these affirmations provide little relief from our loneliness for they seem to be at variance with the facts of our experience. We pray for things. Sometimes we get them and sometimes we don't; it's not a simple matter. Why do we have to pray to a good, all-knowing God anyway? If God knows what we need and is good, why tell him? Doesn't Jesus say in Matthew 6: 8, "Your Father knows what you need before you ask him"?

The issue of biblical prayer is a complicated one. We have to probe deeply if we are to ascertain the wisdom and meaning of prayer. Perhaps the place to begin is a recognition of the complexity of the Bible. Just how do we view the Bible? What part does it play in our life? Some people have used Jesus' words on peace to emphasize pacifism and draft evasion. Others have used the episode in which Jesus took a whip and overturned the tables of the moneychangers to justify war and killing. Biblical interpretation is a crucial matter. It's no less crucial on the issue of prayer life.

If we take out of context the above promises regarding prayer and view them as literal truth in themselves, a very sweet and simple picture of prayer is obtained. But the Bible is also full of unanswered prayer. The prophet complains that inequity and injustice abound in the world, and he wonders just how long he has to pray before God will listen and take action. Moses prayed to enter the promised land, but he died on Mount Nebo. The Book of Lamentations contains the story of a national calamity in which a patriot responds that God covered himself with a cloud so no prayer could get through. Paul prayed many times that a physical handicap called a "thorn in the flesh" which was hurting his ministry would be removed. It was not, and for the rest of his life he simply had to make the best of it. Even Jesus in the Garden prayed for release from his fate but did not receive it. So, if we are looking for an easy formula, a shortcut to answered prayer, let us at least admit that Scripture doesn't offer that.

The prayers of the Bible are intensely individualistic. Paul preferred to pray kneeling; Jeremiah prayed standing; David prayed sitting; Jesus prostrated himself before God. Ezekiel and Isaiah prayed aloud; Hannah prayed silently. There are as many different ways of praying as there are different people. Such recognition can at least alleviate our fear that prayer will not be valid experience if we do not practice prayer the way someone else does.

The Adequacy of Prayer for the Present Age

Most of our disillusionments with prayer, it seems to me, come from our viewing it solely as a means of getting things. We need a new motive for praying. We often pray for miracles that would leave us poorer than we were—miracles like a chance for a better job; relief from nagging backaches and illness; success in love affairs and winning athletic contests. John Killinger is right—"It's on the basis of praying for miracles like these that prayer gets a bad name." [2]

We need a new motive for prayer. But isn't this what new knowledge requires in most of life? For example, men used to put flowers on graves because they thought that the departed spirits enjoyed the odor. That superstition has long been passed but we still put flowers on graves. Sentiment has taken the place of superstition.[3] The motive has been changed. But the practice is perhaps more meaningful than ever.

Let us attempt to understand some new motives for the exercise of prayer. In the first place, consider the *natural-*

ness of prayer. Prayer is a natural function, like breathing and eating, and not an artificial addition. Scripture has long recognized the fact that prayer is not something extra. The Psalmist cried out, "My soul is athirst for God"; that is, there is a universal feeling of God-consciousness. Solomon's prayer at the dedication of the temple in 2 Chronicles 6 takes for granted that any stranger coming from anywhere on earth is likely to be a praying person. Paul noticed in the people of Athens a hunger for God and a prayer and worship of the universal.

Each of us has a tendency to pray. It is a natural function. But if it is not disciplined and understood, it becomes a selfish, unintelligent cry of need. If it is not trained, it becomes a selfish begging when we reach our wit's end. Instead of praying for miracles, then, we need to see the world for what it is, a miracle in itself. Only then can prayer reach its highest form, as gratitude, and our loneliness become dissolved. Prayer is the cultivation of a natural function ingrained in the human spirit to combat the terrors of human loneliness.

I have long contended that much of the loneliness we experience in life we bring upon ourselves.[4] Much of our loneliness results from the feeling of being cut off from a sense of purpose. For the Christian, this ultimate sense of purpose is God. Prayer, then, is a force which enables us to "plug into" the Creator. Most of the time the ways of the world are not God's ways and we stand in direct conflict with secular values and principles. It is a lonely feeling to watch as our world rushes headlong into the nuclear armaments race, experiences increased need for redistribution of the world's wealth, and creates numerous vocational and financial crises that place unprecedented stress on families and individuals. The "foolishness" of the Beatitudes wears heavily upon us. Servanthood becomes more lonely in na-

ture. No politician is ever elected on a platform of shrink-
age, meekness, and redistribution.

Those who embrace the Beatitudes are very much in the
minority. Christianity itself, with all of its emphases on
human rights, is very much a minority religion on the stage
of the world's great religious movements. Sometimes such
minority positioning convinces many that we are without
hope, and that insecurity leads them into criticism of the
very principles of Christianity in order to satisfy their ego.
For example, I once visited a young woman in prison who
related to me that her parents never expressed a kind word
about any of the authority figures in her life. All her life
she had heard the minister, her teachers, the school princi-
pal, the politicians, and other significant adult authority
figures soundly criticized. Naturally, over a period of years
her mind absorbed the negativism and when she became a
young adult she had found no positive valuations. Now,
God is an authority figure. Rather than shrink from such
acknowledgment, I think we should embrace it. Prayer is
actually an effort to acknowledge God as the ultimate authority in life. Consequently it is a process of solidarity in
the face of a lonely stand against the world's values.

Rabbi Abraham Heschel tells a parable about a kingdom
in which the grain crop was poisoned. Everyone who ate
the grain went crazy. But because there were few other food
supplies, the people were faced with eating the grain or
starving. Surveying the situation, the king said, "Very well,
then, let us eat the grain, for we cannot starve. But let us
at the same time feed a few people on a different diet so
we will at least have some people who will know that we are
insane."

The life of prayer differs greatly from the world's materialism. It gives us a way we can remember the source of
our origin and the source into which we die. As our world

continues to eat its food of military hardware, hatred, pornography, and idolatry, some of us must feed on the inner workings of the Spirit of God. It will supply us with the solidarity we need to find meaning and purpose. To form values and purpose and live by them when all others about us are plunging into the chaos of questioning the validity of faith is the value of prayer. The abolitionist Wendell Phillips pointed out the high cost of virtue:

> It is easy to be brave when all behind you agree with you; but the difficulty comes when nine hundred ninety-nine of your friends think you are wrong. Then it is the brave soul who stands up, one among a thousand, remembering that one with God makes a majority.

People who have cultivated the natural function of prayer to combat the terrors of loneliness have in all ages experienced a strength and inspiration that undergirds the Christian way of living.

A second motive for praying is *enhancement of our cooperation with God* in effecting a better world. But we must realize there are three ways in which humans cooperate with God—thinking, working, and praying—and none can take the place of the other. Jesus put it like this: love God with your body, mind, and soul.

We become confused and disillusioned when we ask prayer to do what can be accomplished only through thinking and working. Prayer will not light our homes, tend our gardens, develop our philosophies, and build our cities. Nor will it reach out to others and cultivate new friendships for us, conquer our laziness or improve our vocational performance.

One of the most crucial passages of Scripture for understanding this point is Exodus 14: 15. The Israelites are caught with the Red Sea in front of them and the Egyptians behind them. Moses goes apart to pray. He receives a rather strange reaction from God. *God is angry at Moses for having prayed.* He responds, "Why do you cry to me? Speak to the children of Israel that they will go forward." It's as though God is saying, "I have done everything I can do. It's your move."

Here is a valuable lesson for us—we can't obtain by prayer what comes only as a result of work. Prayer by itself will not compensate for the work outlined in the five previous chapters of this book. Loneliness cannot be conquered by prayer alone. Prayer is a complement to work and thought, not a substitute for them. Jesus himself continuously stressed that a person who cannot forgive his or her brother or sister is not saved.

The Bible seems to indicate that Jesus felt long prayers were a waste of time. He saw people who were too busy being religious to realize that the Kingdom of God had come to them. The Lord's Prayer has only fifty-seven words, fewer than most television commercials. Jesus, too, apparently viewed prayer as a complement to work and thought.

Finally, let us consider as a motive for prayer our quest for *intellectual integrity.* This may seem to be a strange motive for some people. Some people give the impression that we have to forfeit our intellectual integrity to be a follower of Christ. If that were the case, how, then, does prayer facilitate integrity? That is, how does prayer put us in touch with the best that history and psychology have to tell us about the human journey?

The history of the human race is a history of the integrity of prayer. Consider the destruction of the Roman Empire which precipitated the dark ages. The roads had been blocked, the bridges destroyed, the aqueducts cut, the hospitals and libraries burned, and the vast public buildings

changed into homes for squatters. Literacy had become so
rare as to become almost magic. Worldwide law had crum-
bled into the organized gangsterism of the feudal system. In
that setting, monks retired to their coves and in prayer,
thought, and writing, kept the flame of progress flickering
for a better day.[5]

When the Catholic church had become a closed system,
turned in upon itself, a priest named Martin Luther retired
to pray and sensed a vision which propelled the church to
new heights of awareness.

When the dark cloud of slavery hung heavy over our
country, men and women of prayer like Abraham Lincoln,
George Washington Carver, Sojourner Truth and Frederick
Douglas retired to their chambers of prayer and looked for
a better day.

When the barbarism of Nazi Germany swept Europe,
burned its cities and closed its universities, enclaves of the
confessing church in Germany gathered in prayer to keep
alive the vision of a better day. When we pray, we exercise
a phenomenon that touches base with the historical solidarity of the human race. There is more to prayer than the
infantile babblings most of us are accustomed to.

My colleague Paul Hanson is correct—the community of
faith is able to relate historical events and present activity
to an historical heritage which enables us to perceive ourselves as a part of God's purposeful plan for the human race.
Prayer, as part of our heritage, unites us with the movement
of God in human history.

A Collective Unconscious

Virtually every book written on the subject of prayer has
been addressed to the person as if prayer were strictly a

private matter. Yet the early church seemed to focus on prayer explicitly as a communal activity. In fact, the Lord's Prayer seems to be a device aimed at teaching new converts how to pray together.

Belonging to a positive Christian community of prayer is a significant relationship most of us need for combatting loneliness. Our needs as humans have been the object of much clinical study. Few of us like to be compared to rats, but there are many traits we share. In his profound work, *Understanding Prayer,* Edgar Jackson relates that a group of scientists did experiments with rats to determine what gave them a will to live. In one of the experiments they placed healthy rats in vats of water to see how long they could float or swim before they gave up the struggle for life and drowned. The rats swam from sixty to eighty hours before they gave up. A similar group of rats, just as healthy, were placed in similar vats, with one major difference; they had their whiskers cut off. Rats' whiskers, of course, serve as their chief contact with the world about them. They provide sensory clues to the object and spatial relationship between the rats and their world. These rats exhibited quite different behavior. Within ten minutes some of them were dead. None of them showed half the will to live of the first group.[6]

Without overgeneralization, I believe that when relationships and contacts with meaningful things are broken, the will to live is affected in all living creatures.

Today's world is experiencing some tragic personal and social experiences because of the disintegration of meaning in our lives. Many individuals have no greater purpose in life than the accumulation of wealth. They lack significant relationships. Like the rats without whiskers, they have abandoned their values and goals in favor of material gods

that can supply little meaning and purpose beyond themselves. They lay up treasures here on earth that can only
rust or melt away.

One of the "whiskers" or stabilizing elements in the life
of a Christian is the awareness, conscious or unconscious,
of the praying fellowship. Carl Jung, the psychiatrist, noted
that a "collective unconscious" works among us. A "collective unconscious" is a sense that operates among people.
It's like the operative force among birds that we observe
when we see thousands of birds, with no apparent signals
among them, change course and yet leave no one straggling.
They possess a communication that tends to make them one.

I have had several experiences reminding me of that
reservoir of spiritual power that we sense. In the birth of
our son, Scott, there were difficulties and complications
which led to emergency surgery. Now, I have tried to assist
many people in crisis situations. My pastoral counseling
background has been called upon many times to provide
calmness and assurance in crisis situations. But when it became my own family that was involved, I found it was a
totally different matter. To sit there with the doctor in his
surgical garb, sign all those papers and witness my family
going down on an elevator, not knowing whether in a few
hours two people would return, one person, or none at all,
was an incredibly lonely experience. To say the least, my
usual circuits of logic were broken and a rational approach
to existence was beyond me.

But in that experience I felt the presence of the church—
not just the local church I belonged to, but the collective
spirit of religiosity in that city. As I walked semi-aimlessly
down to the hospital chapel, I felt that collective entity.
While I was sitting in the chapel, a colleague, the pastor of
the Methodist church, walked in. He and I were the best
of friends. We had exchanged pulpits on many occasions,

lived in the same neighborhood, and worked together on civic committees. We sat together and talked, but didn't verbalize a prayer because our presence itself was prayer. After half an hour he left to attend to other business. The time was short but it was sufficient. My sense of aloneness was transformed into solidarity. I could sense the prayers of my own church and I could sense the prayers of my Methodist friends. I'm certain that some of the prayers were very sophisticated and others were quite immature. But as I sat there I sensed the collective nature of my life; I was not alone. Even the possibility of death and having to start over seemed to be a reality which could be shared. I was not without my "whiskers." Somehow I began to understand sensory clues and how they can affect the will to live.

How can a person survive without that collective feeling? How can one conquer loneliness and experience Christian living without knowing that kind of praying, hoping community? Isn't life diminished without that prayerful vision of the Kingdom of God, of the lion lying down with the lamb, of nations gathering around the throne of God, of strangers being welcomed so that they give up their strangeness and become a part of the community?

Christianity is daring and creative; it is an adventure. Prayer itself is often a unique adventure of the soul. But that is never the totality of the experience. Constantly we find ourselves with problems that are not adventuresome or even exciting. Often the task is trying to maintain stability, simply holding onto life instead of managing it. Certainly people who cannot gain purpose and control for their lives cannot be venturesome. We need a sense of collective effort to keep us moving forward in a spirit of excitement and joy. A steady diet of television, movies, dramas, books, and personal experiences composed of 50 percent sex and 50 percent violence cannot supply lasting meaning in life. Neither can a steady diet of bodily ills, hospitals, and nursing homes. Only that "collective unconscious," that idea of trust and corporateness is sufficient to order life, give it hope, and conquer loneliness.

Life is not always fair. But, for the Christian, it is a trust and a collective experience. Though we are often tempted to say that nothing is impossible—if you blow hard on your hands and have faith and courage, *that is not a very deep message.* There are times when all of us face defeat. This is one place where Jesus ran into conflict with the traditional aspects of form and ritual in worship. Prayer had degenerated into futile beggings for success and gratitude which served as a thin veneer of whitewash over corruption. But Jesus brought a kind of living that was triumphant, a message that even in defeat people can win the kind of victory that brings hope and meaning to life. He taught that we can shift directions and triumph over life, that outward victory may really be defeat and outward defeat really victory. Yes, he was a far cry from the religious quacks of his time. And he is a far cry from the flagrant excesses spewed forth from some pulpits, glibly promising perfect health or amazing salvation in six easy lessons. The message of Jesus to his contemporaries and to us was one of power, not superficial gimmickry. He unloosed an amazing spiritual camaraderie that can and does revolutionize our relationships with one another.

The early church was a group action, and we, too, would like to feel part of such group action. We have a great zest in our world for positive Christian community. But, tragically, the sense and feeling of community in most of our churches is marred by disharmony and conflict. The congregation that has not suffered at some time from the ugly scars left by aggressive personalities and lack of compassion is indeed fortunate. While we are called to live in love and peace, it is true that the history of the church is charged with accounts of bitter conflict. And too often our attempts at worship are stained with inflated egos and hidden personal agendas. In his book *Zest for Living,* Gaines Dobbins insists that the revival we need all the way from the family to the nation is *"recovery of that quality of sacrificial devotion to the common welfare that characterized the early Christians. . . ."* [7]

Such a renewal can only come through a heightened awareness of the church as a community of prayer. Prayer creates positive Christian community. While it is important to have good preaching, in itself it does not create community which can conquer loneliness. But prayer creates an attitude of cooperation and trust which enables people to hear and respond to good preaching. Without those committed souls who are sacrificially committed to the common welfare, little support is generated. And without that kind of support the best of sermons only sounds like pieces of information or rivers of pious platitudes, and community is not formed. Prayer and fellowship reinforce each other.

Perhaps life does reduce the opportunities we have to experience meaningful relationships and purposeful activity. But for the Christian in touch with the living God, other humans are no longer strangers but neighbors; loving intimacy instead of consumerism characterizes personal relationships; life itself becomes a gift and we can reach out to heal the hurts of the world in the assurance that we are not alone and our efforts are not in vain.

A world suffering from dehumanization and loneliness awaits with eager anticipation the meaning and purpose which our lives can convey. Through the pilgrimage we have shared here the gospel and the package it is wrapped in, the church, can perhaps become good news once again.

Grace and peace can walk with us through life, liberating us from the human trauma that tends to encompass us. In a time when our children are taught by society that acquisition of property, money, and status are the things in life which really count, perhaps we can form ourselves into communities of prayer, action, love, and understanding which will teach them the value of purpose and meaning. Perhaps friendships can replace valium and confidence in the future replace the wrestling with depression on the psychiatrist's couch. Perhaps we can learn to live in our world house without destroying the people who live in it with us.

The Christian faith as lived out in the context of a viable community can liberate us from loneliness.

NOTES

Chapter 1

1. Suzanne Gordon, *Lonely in America* (New York: Simon and Schuster, 1976).
2. See James J. Lynch, *The Broken Heart: The Medical Consequences of Loneliness* (New York: Basic Books, 1977).
3. Raymond Chapman, *The Loneliness of Man* (London: SCM Press, 1963), p. 11.
4. Martin Luther King, Jr., *Where Do We Go from Here?* (New York: Harper & Row, 1976), p. 195.

Chapter 2

1. Peter J. Gomes, "On Being Particular," a sermon preached October 22, 1978, in Duke Chapel, Duke University, Durham, North Carolina.
2. David Neiswanger, quoted in Bruce Larson, *The Relational Revolution* (Waco, Tex.: Word Books, 1976), p. 55.
3. Reuel Howe, *How to Stay Younger While Growing Older* (Waco, Tex.: Word Books, 1976).
4. Paul W. Pruyser, *The Minister As Diagnostician*, p. 78.
5. See Parker J. Palmer, "A Place Called Community,' *The Presbyterian Journal* 94:9 (16 March 1977), p. 252.
6. Walter Rauschenbusch, *Christianizing the Social Order* (New York: Macmillan, 1914), p. 49.
7. New York: Harper & Row, 1976.

8. Irving L. Janis, *Stress and Frustration* (New York: Harcourt, Brace, Jovanovich, 1969).
9. Charles Darwin's *Autobiography*, ed. Nora Barlow (London: William Collins Sons and Company, 1958).
10. Ibid.

Chapter 3

1. David Saville Muzzey, *Ethics as a Religion* (New York: Simon and Schuster, 1951), pp. 32–35.
2. Ibid.

Chapter 4

1. New York: Harper & Row, 1976.
2. Ibid., p. 98.
3. Raymond Chapman, *The Loneliness of Man*, p. 29.
4. As quoted in "Beautiful, Bright, Rich, . . . and Single," *Boston Evening Globe*, 20 June 1973.
5. Charles C. L. Kao, *Search for Maturity* (Philadelphia: Westminster Press, 1975), p. 14.
6. Harry Emerson Fosdick, *The Hope of the World* (New York: Harper, 1933), pp. 39–48. I owe much to Fosdick's sermon "Modern Civilization's Crucial Problem."
7. See Lee Gilbert Highet, *Man's Unconquerable Mind* (New York: Columbia University Press, 1954), p. 17.
8. Quoted by Immanuel Kant in *Observations on the Feeling of the Beautiful and Sublime*, trans. John T. Goldwait (Berkeley: University of California Press, 1960), pp. 48–49.
9. New York: Holt, Rinehart, and Winston, 1977.

Chapter 5

1. Harold C. Warlick, Jr., *Sketches of Creative Living* (Lima, Ohio: C.S.S. Publishing Co., 1977), p. 48.

2. James A. Taylor, "Progency of Programmers: Evangelical Religion and the Television Age," *The Christian Century*, 20 April 1977, pp. 379–82.
3. Paul D. Hanson, *Dynamic Transcendence* (Philadelphia: Fortress Press, 1978), p. 52.

Chapter 6

1. Ernest Becker, *The Denial of Death* (New York: 1973), p. 255.
2. John Killinger, *Bread for the Wilderness/Wine for the Journey* (Waco, Tex.: Word Books, 1976), p. 32.
3. See Harry Emerson Fosdick, *The Meaning of Prayer* (New York: YMCA, 1915), p. 30. This work was pivotal for this chapter's material.
4. Harold C. Warlick, Jr., *Sketches of Creative Living*, p. 38.
5. See Gilbert Highet, *Man's Unconquerable Mind*, pp. 23–24.
6. Edgar N. Jackson, *Understanding Prayer* (New York: World Publishing Co., 1968), pp. 177–78.
7. Gaines S. Dobbins, *Zest for Living* (Waco, Tex.: Word Books, 1977), p. 47.